PICK
POCKET·GUIDE

STAR WARS
TOYS

How to Pick Antiques like a Pro

MARK BELLOMO

Copyright ©2015 Mark Bellomo

All rights reserved. No portion of this publication may be reproduced or transmitted in any form or by any means, electronic or mechanical, including photocopy, recording, or any information storage and retrieval system, without permission in writing from the publisher, except by a reviewer who may quote brief passages in a critical article or review to be printed in a magazine or newspaper, or electronically transmitted on radio, television, or the Internet.

Published by

Krause Publications, a division of F+W Media, Inc.
700 East State Street • Iola, WI 54990-0001
715-445-2214 • 888-457-2873
www.krausebooks.com

To order books, visit us online at www.krausebooks.com

The word STAR WARS and its associated trademarks are owned by Disney/Lucasfilm & licensed to Hasbro, Inc. and are used in this book solely for identification purposes. Disney/Lucasfilm & Hasbro, Inc., assume no responsibility for the content of this book. The publisher is not sponsored by or associated with Disney/Lucasfilm & Hasbro, Inc. or its affiliates. This book is the result of the author's independent research reporting on the secondary market and is intended to provide information for collectors.

Cover photos, top row, from left: Cloud City Playset—P. 42; Yoda action figure—P. 39; R2-D2 action figure—P. 55; Darth Vader large size action figure—P. 30; **bottom row, from left**: Jabba the Hutt Action Playset—P. 44; Tauntaun with Open Belly Rescue Feature (with Luke Skywalker in Hoth Battle gear)—**$175-$195+ MISB, $110-$135+ MIB** (no yellowing to belly), **$65-$85+ MLC** (yellowed belly); Death Star Space Station—**$1,200-$1,400 MISB, $350-$425 MIB, $125-$150+ MLC**.

ISBN-13: 978-1-4402-4582-4
ISBN-10: 1-4402-4582-7

Designed by: Jana Tappa
Edited by: Kristine Manty

Printed in China

10 9 8 7 6 5 4 3 2 1

CONTENTS

ACKNOWLEDGMENTS 4

INTRODUCTION... 5

CH 1: STAR WARS VINTAGE LINE 22

CH 2: THE EMPIRE STRIKES BACK 34

CH 3: RETURN OF THE JEDI 44

CH 4: POWER OF THE FORCE 54

CH 5: POWER OF THE FORCE II 66

CH 6: THE PHANTOM MENACE 94

CH 7: POWER OF THE JEDI 104

CH 8: STAR WARS SAGA 114

CH 9: CLONE WARS 134

CH 10: ORIGINAL TRILOGY COLLECTION . 140

CH 11: REVENGE OF THE SITH 150

CH 12: THE SAGA COLLECTION 162

CH 13: ANNIVERSARY COLLECTION 178

CH 14: SAGA LEGENDS 200

ABOUT THE AUTHOR 208

Acknowledgments

I'd like to thank my gorgeous wife, Jessica Rivers-Bellomo, for her endless support: I adore her. She is my muse and my rock. I can't write a darned word without her by my side. I'm indebted to her for not only allowing me to amass a ludicrous collection of comics and toys, but for taking care of the family (our faithful Maine Coons Pea Pod and Iggy) whenever I crawl down the rabbit hole to write another collectible book.

Also, I'd like to give thanks to my mom and dad for modeling their work ethic and also for never forcing me to "stop collecting those stupid toys," regardless of what anyone said. Like my editorial director, Paul Kennedy (AND my editor Kris Manty, AND Krause's in-house photographer, Kris Kandler), my parents always trusted I that knew what I was doing, even if I didn't really know myself. Without the guidance and unconditional positive regard provided by my mom and dad, none of these books would have ever been possible.

Introduction

The foundation of global popular culture was shaken to its core in 1977 when George Lucas released one of the most important films in modern American history: the science fiction space opera, *Star Wars: A New Hope*.

Over the past 30+ years, eager fans have popularized *Star Wars* terms that have been indelibly stamped onto our collective consciousness and even introduced into the American lexicon: words like "lightsaber," "Jedi Knight," and "droids"; expressions such as "May The Force Be With You," and the moral/psychic concept of "the dark side of the Force." Nearly 100 unique figures were produced in Kenner's vintage *Star Wars* line (discounting the company's *Droids* and *Ewoks* sub-lines released in 1985) between 1978 and 1985. Records show that the company sold almost 300 million action figures in total.

Yet little did 20th Century Fox realize the impact that the film would have on children and adult collectors everywhere, and in a brilliant stroke of prescience, Lucas may have subconsciously realized the potential of the *Star Wars* franchise. Lucas alone contracted to retain all sequel and merchandising rights for the film(s).

Kenner toys obtained the rights to produce 3-3/4-inch action figures, playsets, creatures, and vehicles based on important scenes from *Star Wars*. The smaller 3-3/4-inch scale was utilized in direct response to the OPEC oil shortages of the 1970s, scarcities that increased the cost of plastic production which was affecting many major toy companies such as Hasbro, Fisher Price, and Mego. Little would Kenner realize the overwhelming response that their more portable *Star Wars* figures would attract on retail shelves. Soon after their release, the 3-3/4-inch action figure format would become the standard in the field. At this smaller size (as opposed to Hasbro's enormous 11-1/2-inch G.I. Joe figures or Mego's interchangeable 8-inch figure body), characters were easier to produce, simpler to manufacture, and could ultimately sell higher numbers in order to allow consumers to purchase many more units ("collect them all") — refreshing sold-out retail pegs much more quickly.

Star Wars figures became a sensation — a phenomenon — in the late 1970s/early 1980s, and the items sold briskly throughout the release of the original trilogy, producing a bevy of toys for each of the three films: *A New Hope (Episode IV)*, *The Empire Strikes Back (Episode V)*, and *The Return of the Jedi (Episode VI)*. A total of 96 figures were available in the original "vintage" line (1977-1985), not including myriad figure variations (telescoping light sabers, vinyl-caped Jawas, etc.), or the Sy Snootles and the Rebo Band three-pack set. The most popular and valuable of these carded figures are the earliest *Star Wars* releases, those figures found on original "12-back cards" — those card backs that showed only the first 12 *Star Wars* action figures in 1977. Other pricey figures can be found within the final run of the line, 1984/85's "Power of the Force" collection, where figures (both new sculpts and previously released characters) were carded along with a collector's coin. A few of these carded samples are worth thousands of dollars in Mint on Card (MOC) condition.

Along with the standard 3-3/4-inch figures was a collection of deluxe 12-inch Large Size figures based on more popular characters from the films — these were the first deluxe 12-inch action figures made in the likenesses of the most popular characters from the original *Star Wars* trilogy, and are held in high regard by *Star Wars* aficionados.

Apart from releasing nearly one hundred *Star Wars* action figures, Kenner crafted 5 creatures, 31 vehicles (including store exclusives), 13 playsets (again, including exclusives), a few assorted accessories, and 7 action figure storage cases. Also adding to the collecting fun were assorted ephemera: proof of-purchase mail-aways that children desired, a Collector's Action Stand, an Action Figure Survival Kit, a Display Arena, myriad Power of the Force coins, pack-in posters, and special bagged figures solicited before their official retail carded release. These special offers added an air of anticipation to the hobby of collecting, and most kids couldn't wait for these packages to arrive in the mail: Kenner always treated kids as truly special customers.

Regardless of all of this, the vintage *Star Wars* line was cancelled in 1985 due to poor sales and a shrinking sci-fi marketplace. Sadly, it would be ten long years before *Star Wars* collectors would be treated to any new toys.

To much fanfare, Kenner released a new series of *Star Wars* action figures in 1995, and the "Power of the Force" line (or, as fans dubbed it, the "POTF II" line) was born. Although initially criticized for their bulky statures and poor facial sculpts, the POTF II action figure line lasted five years and yielded many excellent new figures, a slew of unproduced characters, and even improved paint applications, intricate figure sculpts, and added articulation.

From 1995-present, Hasbro — the most recent owner of the *Star Wars* action figure license — has produced many different lines under the *Star Wars* brand: *Shadows of the Empire* (1996); *Episode I* (1999-2002); Power of the Jedi (2000-2002); *Star Wars* Saga (2002-2004); *Clone Wars* (2004-2005); Original Trilogy Collection (2004); *Revenge of the Sith* (2005); The Saga Collection (2006); The 30th Anniversary Collection (2006-2008); [please note that the following lines are not reviewed in this book due to space restrictions] *The Clone Wars* (2008-2013); The Legacy Collection (2008-2011, 2013); the spectacular Vintage Collection (2010-2013); and the brilliantly constructed modern Black Collection (2013-present).

Star Wars toys are some of the most desirable action figures on the secondary market, and the people who collect them are often the most devoted in the hobby. Vintage figures and vehicles still sealed in their packages command outrageous prices on online auction sites such as eBay and in collectible stores, and with the new films on the horizon, don't get caught unawares.

I'm often asked, "Is it too late to start a *Star Wars* collection?"

My continued response is, "of COURSE not."

It's never too late.

I would recommend starting a *Star Wars* collection. Many pieces in the line are relatively inexpensive. Remember, most figures were solicited in the millions over the course of the first eight years of production. I don't recall any friend of mine from the late-seventies/early-eighties who didn't own at least a few *Star Wars* figures. (And then there was the one spoiled kid on the block who had EVERYTHING ... multiple Stormtroopers, every figure, every vehicle, etc.)

That lucky dog.

Starting a Collection

How should you begin collecting? I would recommend you begin pursuing a <u>vintage</u> Star Wars collection. And you could do so with just a few hundred dollars. Take your time. Be patient. Buy items in lots at auctions — because that's where you'll find the deals. If you're beginning a vintage collection, then don't worry so much about buying action figures individually — you'll save fa-a-a-a-ar more money buying any vintage Star Wars toys (action figures, accessories, playsets, vehicles, etc.) in lots. For instance, in order to nab all twelve of the original figures from 1978, it'll cost you roughly $250-$300 (not including shipping) — but it would be 10 to 15 percent cheaper if you buy them in a lot, or as a set. Throw in another $115-$150 for the 1979 series of *Star*

Wars figures (including Boba Fett, of course). And about $725-$900 for all of the Star Wars playsets, vehicles, and accessories (such as the vinyl Mini-Figures Collector's Case). That means if you want to try and acquire every standard piece from Kenner's 1978-79 *Star Wars* product, all in MLC (Mint, Loose, and Complete) condition, it should run you roughly $1,350 at the most. A little over a grand to walk back in time and play with all those toys you owned when you were a kid.

That's awesome.

Of course, that's a grand for the STANDARD stuff. However, if you're looking to branch off into the rarer variations (e.g., a vinyl-caped Jawa [$1,200-$1,500 mint, loose, and complete], Ben or Luke or Darth with double-telescoping lightsabers [$$$$$], a Sand Person with hollow cheek tubes [$90-$120+], the vinyl Mini-Figures Collector's Case with a prototype Boba Fett insert [$200+], or even the less-expensive, small-headed Han Solo variation [$32]) or the catalog-exclusive items (e.g., the Sears exclusive Cantina Adventure Set with the highly prized [and delicately painted] Snaggletooth with blue uniform variation [$325+]). Let's not forget the mail-away items such as the Collector's Action Stand, which was featured as a promotional on action figures' package backs, or the ridiculously expensive Early Bird Kit. If you pursue this stuff, say goodbye to your bank account: you'll be spending thousands of dollars.

And if you're one of those folks who seeks only factory-sealed items ... then you're looking at tens of thousands of dollars. That's why MISB (Mint In Sealed Box) items are so very expensive — because they're quite rare. Back in the late-seventies no one thought to keep a toy intact, pristine and unopened.

But if you're a casual *Star Wars* fan or picker looking to begin a collection, what about keeping it simple? Choose your favorite character, and buy items related to that character. Han Solo comes to mind. Knock off his vintage action figures first; the large- and small-headed variations of the original Han Solo (1978). Then move to his appearances in *The Empire Strikes Back*: Han Solo (Hoth Outfit, 1980), Han Solo (Bespin Outfit, 1980). Next, try out his *Return of the Jedi* offerings: both uniform variations of Han Solo (In Trench Coat, 1984). Then shuffle on to his super hard-to-obtain Power of the Force appearance as Han Solo (In Carbonite Chamber). If you've been bitten by the collecting bug at this point in your pursuit of this new hobby, there's always a bevy of Power of the Force II items to capture. Han Solo (Mynock Hunt). Han Solo (with tauntaun). It's just that simple. Feed your fondness of this iconic toy line however you want. You can collect these figures Mint On Card (MOC), or Mint Loose and Complete (MLC).

There are many ways to begin. And thankfully, there's no wrong or right way to approach the hobby.

How To Use This Book

The following abbreviations will often be used when collectors refer to the six films and other aspects of the *Star Wars* universe comprising the original film trilogies. In this book, distinct assortments of *Star Wars* toys are dubbed "sub-lines." For instance, Luke Skywalker (Jedi Knight Outfit) was produced for the *ROTJ* (*Return of the Jedi*) sub-line, solicited at retail on *Return of the Jedi* packaging from late 1982 until 1984. This *ROTJ* sub-line is part of Kenner's vintage *Star Wars* toy line, yet is so expansive it receives its own chapter.

Unfortunately, because of the vast amount of *Star Wars* product produced during the past (almost) forty years, it's quite difficult to determine exactly what type of toy you're holding.

Abbreviations of the Toy Lines

TPM = *Star Wars: Episode I, The Phantom Menace* (the film [1999] OR the toy line [1999-2000])

AOTC = *Star Wars: Episode II, Attack of the Clones* (the 2002 film)

ROTS = *Star Wars: Episode III, Revenge of the Sith* (the film [2005] OR the toy line [2005-early 2006])

ANH = *Star Wars: Episode IV, A New Hope* (the film [1977] OR the original toy line [labelled "Star Wars"—1978-1979])

ESB = *Star Wars: Episode V, The Empire Strikes Back* (the film [1980] OR the toy line [1980-1982])

ROTJ = *Star Wars: Episode VI, Return of the Jedi* (the film [1983] OR the toy line [late 1982-1984])

POTF = Power of the Force toy line (the final assortment of the vintage *Star Wars* toy line [1984-1985])

POTF II = Power of the Force II toy line (the first assortment produced for the Kenner/Hasbro *Star Wars* renaissance (1995-2000)

POTJ = Power of the Jedi toy line (2000-2002)

SWS = Star Wars Saga toy line (2002-2004)

CW [animated] = *Clone Wars* toy line (2003-2005), animated toy sculpts (based on the 2003 cartoon)

CW [standard] = *Clone Wars* toy line (2003-2005), realistic toy sculpts (based on the 2003 cartoon)

OTC = Original Trilogy Collection toy line (2004-2005)

TSC = The Saga Collection toy line (2006-2007)

TAC = 30th ["Thirtieth"] Anniversary Collection toy line (2007-2008)

SL = Saga Legends toy line (2007-2011)

Expanded Universe

One more important abbreviation that deserves to be defined is "EU," which stands for the *Star Wars* "Expanded Universe." The EU represents officially licensed material that existed outside of the six feature *Star Wars* films (Dark Horse Comics, Bantam novels, LucasArts video games, etc.) and other canonical sources (*The Clone Wars*). Although this material has recently (2015) been branded outside of the established *Star Wars* canon, a tremendous amount of product has been produced over the past forty years.

Variant vs. Variation

Although most collectors use the terms *variant* and *variation* interchangeably, I would suggest that there is a distinct and important difference between the two terms that are used to describe action figures and related items.

A variant is "different; alternative"—I would further suggest that a variant is deliberate. In the action figure industry, with the Toy Biz/Hasbro Marvel Legends super hero line, releasing variant action figures is the norm. Iron Fist with green (standard) and red (variant) costumes. Usually one variant is "short-packed," and hence may command more money on the secondary market than the other. Sometimes it is an even split. Regardless, a variant is a toy that is intentionally solicited in more than one version, but is—in the most technical sense—considered the same toy from a manufacturing standpoint. For instance, the *Star Wars* Saga Endor Rebel Soldier (2002, #33) was sold with a *bearded* head sculpt, and with a *clean-faced* head sculpt. Although each of them counts as an Endor Rebel Solider, there are indeed two different variants of the figure available on the marketplace.

A variation is a bit different and was quite prevalent during the production of Kenner's vintage *Star*

Wars line. A variation is "the act, process, or accident of varying in condition, character, or degree"— and is nearly always accidental. The sewn shut variation or snap-together variation of the robe for Luke Skywalker (Jedi Knight) in the *ROTJ* sub-line. The vinyl-caped Jawa is one of two variations of the small, robed *Star Wars* figure: the other (far more common) variation is the Jawa with a cloth robe. Yoda with an orange snake or a brown snake is another variation—an unintended consequence of producing action figures at many different factories around the world. When these figures are produced in the hundreds of millions, certain factories have run out of a type of cloth, of a color of plastic, or even of a misplaced figure mold, which leads to a quick fix in order to keep up with the demands of the marketplace.

Troop Building

Some collectors are devoted to a particular soldier or trooper group in the *Star Wars* universe, and have decided that one of their goals in the hobby will be to amass a large amount of the soldiers for play or for display purposes. Whether they're searching for dozens of Clone Troopers or hundreds of tan Battle Droids, the term for this is "troop building," and it's practiced quite often in *Star Wars* collecting circles. It's the reason why Hasbro insists on releasing a good amount of generic soldiers in each of their new figure assortments: *Star Wars* diehards love purchasing multiples of their favorite trooper. From Imperial Stormtroopers and Sandtroopers to Biker Scouts and Imperial Gunners, aficionados can't satisfy their urge to build the largest army on the block.

Pricing

The prices listed in this guide are the best assessments available based upon the pricing currently realized via a "Completed Items Search" on eBay, as well as from many prominent retailers across the United States.

> ### Picker's Tip
>
> If you don't have the large bank account required to collect rare and MISB *Star Wars* items, it's best to keep it simple and choose a favorite character, and buy items related to that character.

These prices should be used as a guide only — and as such, can be quickly outdated: please take the pricing in this book with due deference. The prices listed in this guide are for NON-AFA GRADED toys, i.e., pieces that have not been professionally assessed and given a grade by the Action Figure Authority. For the purpose of assigning value to the *Star Wars* toys in this reference book, there are multiple different ways that Kenner and Hasbro packaged these products for solicitation at retail, with a range of grades assigned to each of these package-types.

First, there are *carded* items (aka. those with *carded bubble* packaging) — those *Star Wars* toys released on a carded bubble — essentially a piece of sturdy chipboard or cardboard (called a "card") with a translucent piece of shaped plastic (called a "bubble") attached via glue or paste so that the toy and its requisite accessories are [entirely] visible to the consumer.

MOC (MINT ON CARD)

The original packaging for the toy in question is completely intact: the bubble is in no way removed (or even slightly separated) from the card, and the figure inside is [usually] in C-10, dead mint condition (a solid "10": on a scale of 1 [the lowest, poorest condition] to 10 [the highest, best condition]) due to the fact that the package has never been opened and the toy in question has never been exposed to human hands.

There are a range of different conditions for MOC figures and toys. Usually, most sellers and buyers can agree that this range of condition may be numerated with the numbers 1-10, with "10" existing as the highest, most perfect specimen found, while a score of a "1" indicates a MOC specimen so trashed that you might as well cut the figure off of the card back. So then, MOC toys will range from C-10 (Condition 10 out of 10 — a perfect score) to C-1 (Condition 1 out of 10 — just awful packaging). Most MOC collectors find C-6 to be the lowest acceptable grade when buying — there are some flaws and detractions apparent on the card or bubble, but not enough to make the piece truly non-displayable.

C-10: A dead mint carded specimen. There are no visible detractions whatsoever. This MOC specimen is perfect in every way. C-10 packaging is nearly impossible to achieve, and usually only carded figures removed from sealed factory cases will meet this condition.

C-9: These MOC specimens have some very minor defects, but these imperfections should not be apparent unless the piece is closely scrutinized. From a short distance, this MOC sample looks perfect, with no obvious wear or creasing apparent OR existing. C-9 is usually considered "Near Mint," and is an eminently displayable piece, of course.

C-8: This condition will have some minor defects, but will pass a test for acceptability. What most people consider to be good condition, this card may have some of the package's original gloss missing, but should be without long creases, without bubble yellowing, and without obvious or extensive signs of wear.

C-7: Carded specimens that grade C-7 have some wear and may have some MINOR creasing or a minor corner fold. The slightest hint of bubble yellowing may begin. The bubble can't be cracked and must still be firmly affixed to the card, but the card may now exhibit minor signs of dust or wear. A poorly-removed price sticker may elicit this grade, but nothing should be deliberately removed from the card.

C-6: Now we're getting into the realm of MOC specimens that many collectors would begin to take a pass on. Signs of wear are apparent. The bubble may be yellowing. The bubble still may not be cracked or lifting from the card back, but creases may be more prominent on the packaging now. Corner bends are more pronounced. At this condition, MLC collectors begin to think: "Should I cut this figure off of the card?"

C-5: Obvious signs of wear. Bubble may begin to lift, but NOTHING must be missing from inside the bubble—not the figure or its accessories. The figure inside must not be damaged in any way. There may be a tear in the place where the package hung onto a retail peg. There may be a very pronounced price tag removal from the card front. Still nothing is cut out of the package, but cracking or brittleness may be apparent with the bubble.

C-4: The lowest grade we'll describe in this book. The packaging is still intact, but the bubble may be 1/2 to 3/4 of the way loosened from the card back. There is now danger that the figure may have been either damaged or removed from the package. Cracked bubbles and yellowed bubbles are common in this grade. The card may be quite worn and wrinkled, but still has a stiffness to it. Many collectors will buy figures in this way and, if the bubble is still sealed to the card, they'll open the MOC sample to remove the MLC action figure. Some collectors choose to purchase only C-1 to C-4 MOC figures because they wish to remove these characters from their packaging to ensure absolutely dead mint action figures. Not a bad way to collect MLC specimens, when you think about it.

When describing the prices of *Star Wars* items in this book, individually carded action figures will nearly always appear on MOC packaging. Whether from Kenner's *ROTJ* sub-line (1982-1984) or from Hasbro's OTC sub-line (2004-2005), a carded figure is a carded figure and ascribes itself to the same set of conditions.

Due to the rarity of many MOC *Star Wars* action figures, particularly from Kenner's vintage sub-lines, some unscrupulous dealers will try and pass off "custom-carded" figures as originals. By using a high-quality printer to replicate the detailed graphics onto replica cardstock, and then constructing custom-made, translucent factory bubbles to match the Kenner originals, these two reproduction items were then used to mount a vintage figure onto this reproduction card back. Some sellers — whether intentionally or unintentionally — may try not to pass these repro cards off as original MOC items.

If you're in doubt re: whether or not to purchase a MOC figure because its provenance is in question, please check with an expert, or compare the package to a confirmed original.

MLC (MINT, LOOSE, AND COMPLETE)

The toy in question is without its original packaging, but has every single one of its included parts (e.g., accessories [laser pistols, light sabers, etc.], missiles, or other easily-lost weapons), yet the specimen is in excellent condition: grading at least a C-8.5 out of 10. Due to the fact that beauty is in the eye of the beholder, it's often better to get an impartial observer to take a look at any item before buying or selling the piece: if someone is selling an item, they will sometimes conflate the price of a toy to match the dollar signs feeding their fondest desire; if someone is buying an item, they will often wish to deflate the price of the toy to match the savings that fuels their heart. The truth lies somewhere in the middle. Regardless of what package type you're looking at, I try to let the buyer (or seller) influence my impartiality. When grading loose toys, a collectible is [only] MLC if the toy-in-question is truly <u>mint</u>, <u>loose</u>, and <u>complete</u>. MINT means free of any and all defects. Many times sellers will slap a "MLC" brand onto a toy before checking to see if the artifact is truly 1) in mint condition and free of defects, and 2) equipped with every single piece that the toy should include. I've heard hundreds (thousands?) of stories about people buying a figure labelled MLC just to find out weeks later that the character was missing some essential accessory. Whether buying or selling a MLC piece, do your research.

Furthermore, many collectors will not purchase a *Star Wars* playset, vehicle, or weapon system unless all of its respective labels are applied and *none* are missing, since missing stickers will adversely impact the overall appearance of the toy. Missing labels should be considered when pricing a MLC *Star Wars* collectible.

However, there is one aspect of collecting MLC *Star Wars* items — and vintage items in particular — that has given many action figure aficionados a powerful headache: reproduction (aka. "repro") *Star Wars* parts. Although casual *Star Wars* fans might applaud the availability of repro accessories since these items are far easier-to-find and (usually) cost much less than original *Star Wars* parts, most diehard vintage *Star Wars* collectors, completists, and troop-builders (those collectors who wish to amass a great number of troops to form an army [of Imperial Stormtroopers, TIE Fighter Pilots, Biker Scouts, etc.]), find that reproduction parts have watered down the market. Furthermore, repro parts allow uninformed sellers to "complete" vintage *Star Wars* action figures (and some playsets and vehicles) with repro parts not realizing that these accessories are reproductions, hence selling these toys as MLC when they are anything but.

There are many dozens of tricks, tips, and reference photos cached and spread over hundreds of pages which can illustrate the difference between repro and original *Star Wars* parts (i.e., Artoo Detour's article, "The Float and Drop Test") to new and returning collectors alike, but the sheer page count would run far too high to be dealt with in this book, so I'll leave you with what I consider to be the single most indispensable Internet source for determining the difference between original and repro parts: *The Imperial Gunnery*, the premiere guide to "vintage *Star Wars* weapons and accessories." From Yoda's gimer stick to Luke Skywalker's "double-telescoping" light saber, the specific difference between reproduction parts and original parts is reviewed on *TIG's* website in detail: www.imperialgunnery.com.

MISB (MINT IN SEALED BOX)

The toy in question remains factory-sealed (taped, glued, etc.) with all of its accessories and packaging inserts (unapplied label sheet, instruction sheet, etc.) intact within its unopened, original box. This is the rarest existing condition for a *Star Wars* toy, and as such, a MISB artifact commands *exponentially* higher prices than those previously opened, MIB (Mint In Box), non-factory-sealed specimens. Particularly when dealing with vintage *Star Wars* pieces.

Therefore, MISB samples of toys are holy grails for many collectors, which is why unscrupulous collectible dealers will try to pass off "re-sealed" MIB items as if they *were* MISB. So then, please inspect purported MISB toys very carefully to determine their authenticity. If the artifact in question is a considerably rare piece, you should contemplate having the AFA Authority professionally grade the toy. MISB means FACTORY-SEALED. Not re-sealed by someone else.

MIB (MINT IN BOX)

The original box for the toy is intact (nothing has been cut out or removed, etc. [such as a Kenner proof-of-purchase seal or Hasbro UPC code]), yet the box is *not* factory-sealed (with tape, glue, etc.), but the package has indeed been opened. The toy is placed within the box, and is in excellent condition, possessing all of its respective accessories and accoutrements.

There are a variety of ways for a toy to be considered MIB. For instance, if the box was carefully opened, and the toy is complete — along with all of its packing inserts, unapplied label sheet, protective cardboard dividers, and paperwork — then the toy is considered MIB as well (and *not* MISB). However, for most collectors and retailers and for this grading standards delineated in this guide, it is not necessary for a MIB toy to include all of the toy's respective paperwork as well (e.g., *Star Wars* product catalog, "Warning" or "Important" inserts, paper promotional material, original shipping bag[gie]), etc., although most collectors will pay handsomely for toys that have all of the inserts intact with all of the toy's parts bags sealed. It may not be considered MISB, but "factory-sealed contents" will boost your returns as a seller. To wit: If the seal on a box is broken, then the toy is MIB.

Furthermore, many collectors will not purchase a *Star Wars* playset, vehicle, or weapon system labelled as MIB unless all of its labels are applied and *none* are missing. Missing labels will adversely affect the toy's aesthetics. When calculating a vintage MIB *Star Wars* item, missing labels should be considered.

MISP (MINT IN SEALED PACKAGE)

The toy in question remains factory-sealed (with tape, glue, PVC plastic, etc.) with all of its accessories and packaging inserts within its unopened, original package. Since this is the rarest condition for a vintage *Star Wars* artifact, like MISB toys, MISP toys command *exorbitantly* high prices on the secondary market. The difference between MISP and MISB? MISP packages might not technically be "boxes"—it might be a circular sealed case, etc.

Since MISP samples of vintage *Star Wars* toys are so rare, unscrupulous dealers will often try to pass off "re-sealed" items as if they were MISP. Therefore, please inspect your MISP toys carefully to determine their authenticity. Similar to MISB items, if a MISP *Star Wars* artifact is a considerably rare piece, you should consider investing some money to have the AFA Authority professionally grade the item.

MIP (MINT IN PACKAGE)

When the original package for the toy is completely intact (nothing has been cut out or removed, etc. [such as a Kenner proof-of-purchase seal]), but said package is *not* factory-sealed (with tape, glue, etc.), but the package has indeed been opened, then the toy is considered MIP. Therefore, a MIP toy is placed within the package, and is in excellent condition, possessing all of its respective accessories and accoutrements.

There are a variety of ways for a toy to be considered MIP: If the package was carefully opened, and the toy is complete, along with all of its packing inserts, protective cardboard dividers, unapplied label sheet, instructions and paperwork, then the toy is considered MIP as well (and not MISP). However, for most collectors and retailers and for this grading standards delineated in this guide, it is not necessary for a MIP toy to include all of the toy's respective paperwork as well (e.g., *Star Wars* product catalog, "Warning" or "Important" inserts, paper promotional material, original shipping bag[gie]), etc. Remember, if the seal on a package is broken, then the toy is MIP.

Missing labels will adversely affect the toy's aesthetics. When calculating a vintage MIP *Star Wars* item, missing labels should be considered. Many finicky collectors will not purchase a vintage playset, vehicle, or weapon system labelled as MIP unless all of its labels are applied and *none* are missing.

CHAPTER 1

Star Wars Vintage Line

Star Wars Episode IV: A New Hope (1977) — the epic space opera that launched one of the premiere media franchises in history premiered in theaters on May 25th, 1977 on a budget of $11 million. Although the profound, lasting influence of the *Star Wars* franchise upon the collective consciousness of Generation X (and nearly every generation since) may never be accurately assessed, *Episode IV's* runaway success at the box office took the many hard-working people who were involved in *A New Hope's* production by surprise.

At the outset, some of those involved with *Episode IV* considered the movie "weird" and a "children's film"; they were put off by the more fantastic elements of the plot introduced by writer/director George Lucas.

Not even toy companies believed in the property. When Lucas originally shopped around the license to

---

Millennium Falcon, 1979, Kenner, *Star Wars* [*A New Hope*], **$150-$185+ [working electronics] MLC**. For many decades, you could find this iconic vehicle/playset for between **$65-$75 mint, loose, and complete**. During the course of the past year, nearly every vintage *Star Wars* toy has endured a ludicrous degree of resurgent interest—unmatched on the secondary market since the collectors' market began. From now on, expect to pay a minimum of $150 a pop for a mint condition, complete Millennium Falcon. When purchasing loose samples, make sure the toy includes its oft-missing radar dish, glossy black "Light Saber Ball" with string and rod, and Dejarik (holochess) table. You should also pop in some batteries to ensure that the starship's working electronics still issue forth a "Battle Alert" sound. Other values for Han Solo's trusty Corellian light freighter? **$2,800-$3,200 MISB** (*Star Wars* packaging); **$275-$305+ [working electronics] MIB**; **$195-$210+ [non-working] MIB**; **$50-$75 [non-working and/or incomplete] MLC**.

produce toys, none of the major buyers bought on the film. Only Kenner Toys — a subsidiary of the Fortune 500 food processing company, General Mills, Inc. (i.e., part of the company's toy division) — bit on the license. This is why the large capital, cursive "G" that represented a General Mills brand was emblazoned on every *Star Wars* toy's proof-of-purchase seal, with the initial line's production.

However, following the film's premiere in the early summer of 1977, *Star Wars* was a bona fide hit with moviegoers and reaped worldwide box office receipts of more than three-quarters of a billion dollars.

But in spite of the runaway success, Kenner severely underestimated consumer demand for merchandise, and did not develop an action figure line quickly enough for a Christmastime 1977 release on store shelves, so one of the company's executives, Bernard Loomis (a man

responsible for some of the most important decisions in the toy industry for many decades) made a stunning decision: to afford kids and collectors the mere PROMISE of action figures to come. Kenner's postponement yielded collectors their first *Star Wars*-related *product* — not of action figures or poseable creatures or deluxe playsets, mind you — but a sort of chipboard "place holder" to placate rabid fans until toy factories finished production on the first assortment of the original twelve action figures, which hit retail shelves in 1978.

Action figures

» 1977, MULTI-PACKS
- Early Bird Kit; mail-away exclusive run by Kenner: includes Luke Skywalker, Princess Leia Organa, R2-D2 and Chewbacca; figures shipped in 1978

» 1978 — 12-BACK CARDS
- Artoo-Detoo (R2-D2)
- Ben (Obi-Wan) Kenobi* (gray or white hair)

- Chewbacca (black [standard] or dark green [early release] bowcaster variations)
- Darth Vader*
- Death Squad Commander ("Star Destroyer Commander" on later *ESB* and *ROTJ* cards)
- Han Solo (large head)
  » *(small head)*
- Jawa (cloth cape)
  » *(vinyl cape)*
- Luke Skywalker* (yellow hair — common)
  » *(brown hair — uncommon)*
- Princess Leia Organa
- C-3PO (See-Threepio)
- Sand People (Tusken Raider)
- Stormtrooper/Imperial Stormtrooper

* The three figures that came complete with telescoping lightsabers (Ben Kenobi, Darth Vader and Luke Skywalker) were also released with double 'telescoping'

Luke Skywalker, 1978, **$450-$750+ MOC** (late-released 12 back SW card), **$30-$40+ [blond hair]**; **$80-$90+ [brown hair] MLC**. The most iconic of all vintage *Star Wars* action figures, the original Luke Skywalker — in collectors' circles known as "Farm Boy Luke" — will always be in high demand, particularly for MOC samples of the earliest-released packages. Called 12-back cards due to the fact that only 12 figures are pictured on the package back, these packaged figures may sell for as high as $750. The sample you see is a later-edition 12-back card featuring the Boba Fett mail-away offer, and it most recently sold for $500 in a similar condition. However, loose collectors shouldn't shy away from purchasing samples of our favorite moisture farmer—but remember: CONDITION IS EVERYTHING: MLC samples of the original blond-haired Luke (with no sun yellowing or damage whatsoever) sell for **$30-$40+** and upward depending on condition. When found with brown hair, he can fetch **$80-$90+** since this variation is a bit rarer. Some advice? If the figure looks like you JUST removed it from its package, then it's in mint condition—any hint of wear or damage will decrease its value. A speck, a ding, a dent—a color rub. ANYTHING. Remember: just because you want a figure to be valuable, doesn't necessarily mean that your hopes will be realized. I've been disappointed myself more often than not.

lightsabers — lightsabers that extended twice. These impossibly rare action figure accessories are quite difficult to obtain and command prices a hundred times (sometimes a thousand times) more expensive than the price of their standard-issue mint, loose, complete counterparts. Luke Skywalker with telescoping saber sells for $185 loose, complete, and $3,200-$3,500 MOC; yet the other two garner much higher prices!

The rarer variant of the Jawa is the version with a vinyl cape (similar to those possessed by Ben [Obi-Wan] Kenobi, Darth Vader, Princess Leia Organa, and the Sand People) instead of a cloth cape. Beware of dealers offering Jawas with vinyl capes, as these are impossible to find and are usually reproductions. Try to have the vinyl caped Jawa authenticated by a reputable dealer prior to purchase. You see, actual vinyl-caped Jawas sell for THOUSANDS Mint On Card, and more than a grand for mint, loose and complete specimens.

» **1978/EARLY 1979— 20 & 21-BACK CARDS**
- Arfive-Defour (R5-D4)
- Death Star Droid
- Greedo
- Hammerhead
- Luke Skywalker X-Wing Pilot
- Power Droid
- Snaggletooth
- Walrus Man
- Boba Fett (mailer box or MOC)

The Snaggletooth that was released MOC was the shorter

maroon-costumed version of the character. The rare and quite expensive Sears Exclusive Cantina Adventure Playset [made of chipboard] included four denizens of the famous Creature Cantina: Greedo, Hammerhead, Walrusman, and Snaggletooth — yet a *taller* Snaggletooth with a blue costume. (This "blue" Snaggletooth is in high demand, commanding prices upwards of $ and more).

As one of the most popular *Star Wars* characters ever, Boba Fett — a Mandalorian bounty hunter who only spoke a total of 27 words in the entire original trilogy — has become a high-demand action figure. However, like the vinyl-caped Jawa, Boba Fett was *never* released with his "rocket-firing backpack" in ANY way to the general public due to a child choking on the small missile of a Mattel *Battlestar Galactica* toy: Kenner feared that the miniscule size of Boba Fett's rocket would lead to a choking hazard. These Boba Fett figures with missile firing backpacks only show up as prohibitively expensive Kenner prototypes (think: the cost of a low-end brand new car) — so then, buyers beware! If you manage to track one down, have it verified by a reputable dealer.

Han Solo, 1978, **$385-$410+ MOC** (*ESB* card), **$15-$20+** [large head]; **$25-$32+** [small head] MLC. One of the more fascinating aspects of the vintage Kenner line is the ability for multiple factories to produce different-looking figures. Without getting into the nuanced "COO" debate (variations of figures based on Country of Origin), there are still some major variations that translate to different prices for the same action figure release. Here is the original Han Solo action figure, who can be found with a "small head" (earliest releases [left]) or "large head" (most later releases [right]). Since there were more "large-head" Han Solo figures produced, and the fact that the "smaller headed" Hans are more aesthetically-pleasing, this variation is more expensive on the secondary market.

» 12" LARGE SIZE ACTION FIGURES

- Ben (Obi-Wan) Kenobi
- Boba Fett (*Star Wars* packaging)
- C-3PO
- Chewbacca
- Darth Vader
- Han Solo
- Jawa
- Luke Skywalker
- Princess Leia Organa
- R2-D2
- Stormtrooper

Accessories
- Collector's Action Stand (mail-away)

Carrying cases
- *Star Wars* (vinyl) Mini-Figures Collector's Case [holds 24 figures]

Creatures
- Patrol Dewback

Sand People, 1978, **$250-325+ MOC** (earlier-released SW card); **$125-$160+ MOC** (later-released ESB card). Many casual collectors are unaware of an important aspect of collecting boxed or carded vintage *Star Wars* toys: Packaging is everything. Not just the condition of the package, but the date the package was released as well. Most of the time, purchasing a vintage action figure, creature, playset, vehicle, or weapon system within the package that artifact was originally released is your best bet, and commands the most money on the secondary market. For instance, buying a MOC Sand People/Tusken Raider action figure on its original 12-back *Star Wars* card is more valuable than if you'd nabbed the character on a later-released package from *The Empire Strikes Back*.

Playsets
- Cantina Adventure Set (with Greedo, Hammerhead, Snaggletooth [blue or red colored], Walrus Man) (Sears exclusive)
- Creature Cantina Action Playset
- Death Star Space Station
- Droid Factory
- Land of the Jawas Action Playset

Vehicles
- Darth Vader Tie Fighter
- Imperial TIE Fighter
- Imperial Troop Transporter
- Land Speeder
- *Millennium Falcon*
- Radio Controlled Jawa Sandcrawler (battery-operated)
- Sonic Controlled Land Speeder (battery-operated) (JC Penney exclusive)
- X-wing Fighter

Snaggletooth [red jumpsuit], **$8-$10 MLC**; Snaggletooth [blue jumpsuit], **$200-$240+ MLC** (and more for dead mint samples). Snaggletooth was released by Kenner in two different manifestations: in his more common, smaller, shorter size, sporting a red jumpsuit, and in his more uncommon, larger, taller size, donning a blue-colored jumpsuit. This larger Snaggletooth could only be obtained through Sears' Christmas catalog in a two-pack set, or with the Sears exclusive Cantina Adventure Set and hence is far more expensive.

Boba Fett, 1979, Kenner *Star Wars*, [*The Empire Strikes Back* (*Star Wars Holiday Special*)], **$320-$340** (mailer box, opened; contents sealed) MIB. This photo shows the manner in which Boba Fett and every other mail-away Kenner release was originally solicited: via a white mailer box, with the figure wrapped in a baggie (with accessory), a pamphlet describing said character's place in the *Star Wars* canon, and (often) a Kenner product catalog featuring all of the *Star Wars* toys available at the time. The value of these items increase if they are found still sealed within an entirely unopened original white mailer box—a difficult task to accomplish. A factory-sealed Boba Fett in mailer box could fetch sums in the neighborhood of **$875-$950 MISB**.

Large size action figures, 1979, Kenner *Star Wars* [*A New Hope*]: Darth Vader, **$55-$70+ MLC**; Princess Leia, **$90-$110+ MLC**; Luke Skywalker, **$75-$100 MLC** (depending upon condition of clothing). The foot-tall range of deluxe "Large Size" Action Figures were solicited by Kenner toward the tail end of their *A New Hope* product offerings. Capturing the essence of nearly every major character from Episode IV (and two gleaned from *ESB*), these action figures were a fan's dream come true. But be VERY careful when purchasing loose samples. Over time, the soft plastics utilized to produce the boots and other soft good accoutrements have degraded a bit—so please be cautious when nabbing any specimen with boots (Obi-Wan Kenobi, Han Solo, Luke Skywalker, or Princess Leia Organa), particularly when this footwear has been placed onto a figure's bare "skin." In light of the toys' delicate conditions, the prices for the three figures are delineated as follows: Darth Vader: **$525-$560+ MISB**; **$135-$150 MIB**; **$55-$70+ MLC**; Princess Leia: **$320-$340+ MISB**; **$150-$160 MIB**; **$110-$120 MIB** [with all accessories + "Hairstyle" booklet]; **$90-$110+ MLC** [with all accessories + "Hairstyle" booklet]; **$50-$65+**; hairstyle booklet alone **$20-$22**; Luke Skywalker—**$575-$625+ MISB**; **$145-$165 MIB**; **$75-$100 MLC** [depending upon condition].

Boba Fett, 1979, Kenner *Star Wars* [*The Empire Strikes Back* (*Star Wars Holiday Special*)], **$25-$32 MLC**. One of the oft-repeated (yet apocryphal) stories in the annals of *Star Wars* toy collecting is that a small amount of "rocket firing" mail-away Boba Fett action figures were shipped to fans, since a few collectors misremember possessing a rocket-firing version of the galaxy's most feared bounty hunter. Unfortunately, because Mattel's missile-firing *Battlestar Galactica* Colonial Viper had caused the death of an eight-year-old) with its tiny red projectiles in 1978, this prompted a recall of two million BSG toys—and a modification of the Kenner Boba Fett's rocket-firing backpack ... BEFORE HONORING ANY MAIL AWAY REQUESTS. As a result, every mail-away Boba Fett had this rocket glued into a socket within the figure's back. Therefore, working, rocket-firing samples of Boba Fett did not make it to the general public via retail or mail-away release: any extant rocket-firing sample is either a preproduction piece originating from the hands of a Kenner employee, or is a reproduction piece produced within the last decade for adult collectors only; neither are given a value in this tome. Carded specimens of Boba Fett are in high-demand and are exceedingly rare, with MOC samples fetching the following prices: **$2,700-$3,200+** (*SW* card); **$1,150-$1,450+** (*ESB* card); **$425-$475+** (*ROTJ* card).

Patrol Dewback, 1979, Kenner *Star Wars*, [*A New Hope*], **$165-$190+ MISB**; **$80-95+ MIB**; **$38-$45+ MLC**; Imperial Stormtrooper, 1978, Kenner *Star Wars*, [*A New Hope*], **$15-$22+ MLC** [based upon whiteness of plastic]. The first creature offered in Kenner's vintage *Star Wars* line was the beast of burden dubbed the Patrol Dewback, a massive reptile utilized by Stormtroopers on Tatooine while they hunted for the Death Star plans.

Cantina Adventure Set (pictured above), late 1978, Kenner *Star Wars*, [*A New Hope*] (Sears exclusive), and the Creature Cantina Action Playset (pictured at right), 1979, Kenner *Star Wars*, [*A New Hope*]. When Kenner released its first four denizens of Chalmun's Spaceport Cantina in 1979, these characters could be utilized within these two completely different *Star Wars* play environments: the Sears exclusive chipboard Cantina Adventure Set (released in Christmas of 1978) which was constructed in a manner similar to a pop-up book—and contained the rarer blue Snaggletooth along with the other three figures, and the widely-solicited Creature Cantina Action Playset (1979) that did not include any action figures, yet thrilled the imaginations of many *Star Wars* fans with its many fabulous action features. The Sears exclusive Cantina Adventure Set commands different prices in various conditions: **$1,100-1,350+ MISB**; **$390-$435+ MIB** [with blue Snaggletooth]; **$175-$200+ MIB** [with red Snaggletooth]; **$310-$325 MLC** [with blue Snaggletooth]; **$85-$110+ MLC** [with red Snaggletooth]. The more commonly released Creature Cantina is far more reasonable: **$450-$510+ MISB**; **$100-$120+ MIB**; **$35-$45 MLC**.

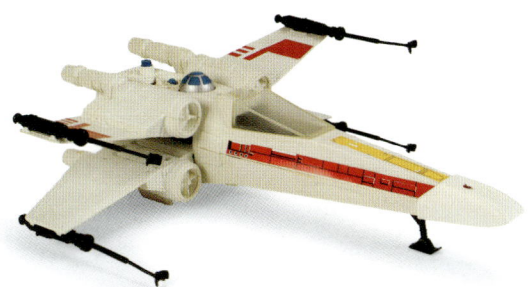

X-wing Fighter, 1978, Kenner *Star Wars*, [*A New Hope*]: **$550-$575+ MISB** (*Star Wars* packaging); **$140-$155+ MIB** [working electronics]; **$115-$130+ MIB** [non-working]; **$85-$100+ MLC** [working electronics]; **$50-$75 MLC** [non-working and/or incomplete].

[Imperial] TIE Fighter, 1978, Kenner *Star Wars*, [*A New Hope*]— **$550-$575+ MISB** (*Star Wars* packaging); **$145-$160+ MIB** [working electronics]; **$115-$130+ MIB** [non-working]; **$80-$95+ MLC** [working electronics]; **$45-$55+ MLC** [non-working and/or incomplete].

CHAPTER 2

Luke Skywalker (Bespin Fatigues), 1980, **$375-$400+ MOC** (brown hair); **$275-$325+ MOC** (blond hair); **$18-$24 MLC** (blond or brown hair variations). This figure possessed a newly designed toy lightsaber far different from the standard "telescoping" lightsabers of the earlier action figure assortment. With a buttoned hilt, this accessory was more aesthetically pleasing than Luke's original accessory. However, as a matter of clarity, the color of Luke's original lightsaber in *A New Hope* and *The Empire Strikes Back* was blue. Unfortunately, Kenner made Luke's first two toy lightsabers yellow.

The Empire Strikes Back

Yet again, the battle to save the cosmos from the evil Darth Vader raged on in the 1980 *Star Wars* sequel, *The Empire Strikes Back*.

While Han Solo, Chewbacca, and Princess Leia busy themselves fending off an attack by the Imperial Army and its All Terrain Armored Transport (AT-AT) Walkers — and then plotting an assault on an Imperial bunker, Luke Skywalker seeks out the ancient Jedi, Grand Master Yoda, to learn the secrets he will require when the dark side of the Force beckons him in a destiny-defining duel with Darth Vader — a duel that ends in a shocking secret that left us moviegoers gasping when we learned who Luke's father really was. How could children of the '80s not want to reenact scenes from what many consider to be the most important film they ever witnessed?

Luckily, Kenner knew kids would want to do just that and came out with a line of action figures, vehicles, creatures, playsets, and accessories that included the Darth Vader Star Destroyer, with an opening and closing light-up meditation chamber, an opening escape hatch, and a pretend viewing screen so Vader could talk to the "Grand Vizier" (the Emperor wasn't named at the time of the toy's release). With pegs on its ceiling to "hang" action figures upside down, Vader could interrogate a suspended Star Destroyer Commander, rather than the un-p.c. "Death Squad Commander."

I never seemed to have enough money for an AT-AT in spite of my paper routes, so I never bought one or its command crew until many years later. I truly had to use my imagination to reenact the Imperials' attack on ice planet Hoth, miming the many Imperial walkers and the flight of fully loaded Rebel Transports that played out the exodus of the Rebels.

Action Figures

» 1980-1981—31, 32, AND 41-BACK CARDS

- AT-AT Commander
- AT-AT Driver
- Bespin Security Guard (Caucasian)
- Bespin Security Guard (African-American)
- Bossk (mailer box or MOC)
- Dengar
- FX-7 (Medical Droid)
- Han Solo (Bespin Outfit)
- Han Solo (Hoth Battle Gear)
- IG-88 (Bounty Hunter) (silver or gray variations)
- Imperial Commander (skinny or round head variations)
- Imperial Stormtrooper (Hoth Battle Gear)
- Lando Calrissian (teeth or no teeth variations)
- Luke Skywalker (Bespin Fatigues) (yellow or brown hair variations)
- Leia Organa (Bespin Gown) (gold/green neck variation)
- Lobot
- Princess Leia Organa (Hoth Outfit)
- Rebel Commander
- Rebel Solider (Hoth Battle Gear)

Bespin Security Guard (I: first release, with moustache [Caucasian]), 1980, Kenner *Star Wars*, [*The Empire Strikes Back*], **$115-$125+ MOC; $8-$10 MLC**. Bespin Security Guard (II) (second release [African-American]), 1981, Kenner *Star Wars*, [*The Empire Strikes Back*], **$100-$110+ MOC; $10-$12 MLC**. One of the very first variants produced by Kenner was that of the Bespin Security Guard (I), a Caucasian trooper solicited in the 1st Wave of 1980's *The Empire Strikes Back* assortment. An all-new sculpt was created for 1981's 3rd Wave—when another Bespin Security Guard (II), an African-American character, was solicited at retail.

- Two-Onebee (2-1B) (metallic or 'flat' paint variations)
- Ugnaught (purple or blue apron variations)
- Yoda (orange or brown snake variations)

» **1981-1982—45, 47, 48-BACK CARDS**
- Artoo-Deeto (with Sensorscope)
- 4-LOM (mailer box or MOC [misidentified (actually the alien Zuckuss)])
- Imperial Tie Fighter Pilot
- Luke Skywalker (Hoth Battle Gear)
- C-3PO [See-Threepio] (with Removable Limbs)
- (Twin-Pod) Cloud Car Pilot
- Zuckuss (misidentified [actually the droid 4-LOM])

» **12" LARGE SIZE ACTION FIGURES**
- Boba Fett (ESB box)
- IG-88

Carrying Cases
- Darth Vader Collector's Case [holds 31 figures]
- Empire Strikes Back (vinyl) Mini-Figure Collector's Case [holds 24 figures] [three different styles]

Creatures
- Hoth Wampa
- Tauntaun (solid belly)
- Tauntaun with Open Belly Rescue Feature

Mini-Rigs & Accessories
- CAP-2
- INT-4
- MLC-3
- MTV-7
- PDT-8
- Radar Laser Cannon
- Tri-Pod Laser Cannon
- Vehicle Maintenance Energizer

Playsets
- Cloud City Playset (Sears Exclusive; with Lobot, Han Solo Bespin Outfit, Dengar, and Ugnaught)
- Dagobah Action Playset
- Darth Vader's Star Destroyer Action Playset

Lando Calrissian, 1980, Kenner *Star Wars*, [*The Empire Strikes Back*], **$150-$165+ MOC** [white teeth variation]; **$10-$14 MLC**. The charming and sophisticated gambler, smuggler, and Baron Administrator of Cloud City, fan-favorite Lando Calrissian has always been a brisk seller on the secondary market—whether or not you'd like your action figure version of him to possess a toothy grin on not (as shown on the carded sample).

- Hoth Ice Planet Adventure Set
- Imperial Attack Base Playset
- Rebel Command Center Adventure Set (Sears Exclusive; with R2-D2 [sensorscope], Luke Hoth and AT-AT Commander)
- Turret and Probot Playset

Vehicles/Accessories
- Action Figure Display Arena (mail-away)
- Action Figure Survival Kit (mail-away)
- AT-AT (All Terrain Armored Transport)
- "Battle-Damaged" X-wing Fighter
- Imperial Cruiser (Sears exclusive)
- Rebel Armored Snowspeeder
- Rebel Transport Vehicle
- Scout Walker Vehicle
- *Slave I*
- Rebel Armored Snowspeeder
- Twin-Pod Cloud Car

Yoda, 1980, Kenner *Star Wars*, [*The Empire Strikes Back*], **$160-$175+ MOC** [orange snake variation]; **$35-$42 MLC** [orange snake variation]. With a few different variations (the main one being Yoda's orange vs. brown snake accessories), the tremendous popularity of this diminutive Jedi Master has endured for more than three decades. While casual collectors will recognize the snake accessory as the action figure's standard variation, there are many more to pursue as you get deeper into the hobby—from different colors of Yoda's body sculpts, multiple eye shades, skin color paint, variations of his Gimer stick and belt, and even dissimilar material for his cream-colored Jedi robe. However, if you're looking for the brown snake variation, then: **$185-$200+ MOC**; **$40-$45 MLC**.

See-Threepio (C-3PO) (with Removable Limbs), 1982, **$10-$14 MLC** (based upon condition of chrome). With his vac-metallized finish and sturdy black plastic backpack which allowed other figures (specifically Chewbacca [who is pictured on the figurine's package front]) to carry the protocol droid, collectors responded well to this new version of the gold protocol droid. Since this was the last version of C-3PO to be sold before 1985's Droids sub-line, there remains quite a bit of demand for this figure MOC, where it sells for **$165-$180**.

Dagobah Action Playset, 1981, **$140-$155+ MIB** [foam in good condition]; **$95-$115+** [foam is degraded]; **$70-$85+ MLC** [foam in good condition]; **$45-$60+ MLC** [foam is degraded]. Perhaps the most impressively action-packed of any vintage *Star Wars* playset, the Dagobah playset truly captures the spirit of Yoda's home and Luke's training ground. From the bark-like details the toymakers etched onto the massive tree stump to Kenner's ability to accurately capture the textures of a swamp that surrounded and encompassed Yoda's Hut, this playset has myriad action features. Collectors could "recreate Darth's and Luke's Lightsaber battle with these action levers," they would be able to "help Luke master 'The Force' with the 'levitation' action lever," "help Yoda to teach Luke to become a Jedi Knight," or even "pretend to lose your action figure and cargo" in the playset's foam swamp, which degrades easily over time. Factory-sealed samples sell for nearly **$500 MISB**.

IG-88 (Large Size Action Figure), 1980, **$265-$290 MLC**. Towering at 15" tall, the assassin droid known as IG-88 is the hardest-to-find of all Large Size *Star Wars* action figures. With his BlasTech DLT-20A Blaster Rifle (the longer armament of the two), his BlasTech E-11 Blaster Rifle, and an E-11 bandolier holster that holds four (4) small red mines, IG-88 was far more intelligent and adept at combat than those garden-variety battle droid[s] that came before him. Due to the character's popularity (and the toy's scarcity), boxed samples are rather high: **$1,450-$1,600+ MISB; $565-$610+ MIB**.

AT-AT [Imperial] All Terrain Armored Transport, 1981, **$135-$155 MLC** [working electronics]; **$125-$140 MLC** [non-working]. This Kenner toy possesses myriad action features: collectors could place AT-AT Drivers in the control room, swivel the machine guns to defend the AT-AT, and activate the vehicle's pulsating, and flash laser cannons to destroy the Rebel Base by pushing the action button. Factory-sealed and boxed samples of this toy fetch high prices: **$825-$975+ MISB**, and **$190-$205+ MIB** [with working electronics]; **$160-$185 MIB** [with non-working electronics].

[Hoth] Wampa, 1982, **$60-$72+ MIB; $26-32+ MLC** [based upon whiteness of plastic]. While Kenner's 6" figure of the ice planet Hoth's Wampa monster pretty accurately captured the beast's size and girth, the creature's facial sculpting was singular: more similar to a wizened old man than that of the ravenous beast featured in *The Empire Strikes Back*. Factory-sealed versions of this creature sell for between **$235-$250+ MISB**.

Cloud City Playset, 1981 (1980 Sears Wish Book), (Sears exclusive), **$130-$165+ MIB** [with four figures]; **$90-$120+ MIB** [without figures]; **$65-$82 MLC** [with four figures]; **$50-$65+ MLC** [without figures]. Tracking down vintage *Star Wars* toys that were exclusively offered to brick-and-mortar department stores or via Christmas catalogs is an exciting prospect for many aficionados: one of the rare opportunities to purchase *Star Wars* toys your local shops might not ordinarily carry: In this instance, Sears, Roebuck, and Company's pop-up chipboard Could City Playset. Solicited in Sears' *Wish Book* in the holiday season of 1980 (packaged with four *ESB* figures: Han Solo in his Bespin Outfit, Dengar, Lobot and Ugnaught), collectors were provided with hours of fun playing with the only toy that allows them to recreate Han Solo being placed into the Carbon Freezing Chamber. And as such, factory-sealed samples of this playset are prohibitively expensive: **$1,100-$1,350+ MISB**.

42 PICKER'S POCKET GUIDE: **STAR WARS TOYS**

Slave 1, Boba Fett's Spaceship, 1981, **$65-$80+ MLC**; **$105-$125+ MIB**; **$975-$1,100 MISB**. Kenner's brilliant *Slave 1* toy possesses a ludicrous amount of special features such as "gravity operated wings... [that] automatically rotate between landing and flight positions," "[a] removable side panel to position Boba Fett for 'take-off' in his remotely operated, clicking pilot seat," twin positionable cannons, an opening (and oft-missing) rear ramp, and a [simulated] 'frozen' Han Solo. The *Slave 1* is truly a magnificent spaceship that still retains its popularity today.

Darth Vader's Star Destroyer Action Playset, 1980, **$145-$170+ MIB** [working electronics]; **$95-$115 MIB** [non-working]; **$58-$75 MLC** [working electronics]; **$45-$55 MLC** [non-working]. Many scenes in *ESB* take place on the deck of Darth Vader's *Executor* (and therefore, this Kenner playset): the recruitment of bounty hunters 4-LOM, Boba Fett, Bossk, Dengar, IG-88, and Zuckuss, Darth Vader utilizing the rejuvenating effects of his specially-crafted spherical hyperbaric meditation chamber, the Sith Lord using his HoloNet transceiver projection pod (on the toy, a translucent flip-down "hologram" screen) for communicating with the Emperor, and also, Vader choking the life out of the incompetent Admiral Ozzel via viewscreen—to show filmgoers his limitless power. Therefore, this is a popular playset on the secondary market, with sealed samples commanding **$550-$610 MISB**.

PICKER'S POCKET GUIDE: **STAR WARS TOYS** 43

CHAPTER 3

Return of the Jedi

In *Return of the Jedi*, the final chapter of the original *Star Wars* trilogy (*Episodes IV-VI*), children of the 1980s witnessed the conclusion of the most important cultural touchstone of Generation X. Most importantly, patient *Star Wars* aficionados finally had the chance to observe Darth Vader's true face: that of former Jedi Knight, Anakin Skywalker. Realizing that the Emperor's right-hand man, Darth Vader, was not beyond redemption — thanks to the faith and encouragement of his son, Luke Skywalker — placed an entirely new importance and added depth to the series: Anakin Skywalker was indeed the "Chosen One" of the ancient Jedi prophecy.

Although a few select "Ewok bashers" crawled out of the woodwork to criticize this tribal community of teddy-bears, we must remember that *Return of the Jedi* was released during a time of contentment for *Star Wars*

Jabba the Hutt Action Playset, 1983. One of the most popular toy playsets ever produced, it commands the following prices on the secondary market: **$235-$275+ MISB** [four-color box]; **$170-$180+ MISB** [catalog release, two-color box]; **$75-$90+ MIB** [four-color box]; **$60-$78+ MISB** [catalog release, two-color box]. With the Jabba the Hutt Action Playset, collectors can thrill to twist Jabba's waist and watch the creature's tail knock over opposing action figures. Kids can toss Jabba's enemies through the flip-up throne/prison doors and onto the bone-ridden floor of the imaginary dungeon below. Fans can pose the cackling Salacious Crumb on the side of throne, allowing the caustic imp to laugh at Jabba's doomed prisoners. Finally, aficionados can accurately pose the obese crime lord to draw at his hookah pipe, sending the Hutt into an intoxicated delirium.

fans. Regardless of how pundits and zealots received the new trilogy of "prequels" (*Episodes I-III*), it's worth noting the astronomical amount of money that rabid *Star Wars* collectors dump into "modern" (1995-present) and "vintage" (1978-1985) product. The current market for vintage *Star Wars* toys is truly obscene: high-grade, investment-quality items are now selling for five to ten times what they were just a few short years ago.

Nonetheless, *Return of the Jedi* provided enthusiasts of the space opera with an epic conclusion to George Lucas' original three-part story arc, and Kenner produced its respective toy line from 1983-84.

Action Figures

» 1983—65, 66, 77, 79-BACK CARDS

- Admiral Ackbar (mailer box or MOC)
- Bib Fortuna (beware of 'red cloaked' Bib Fortunas, as these were not readily available to the public)
- Biker Scout
- Chief Chirpa
- 8-D8
- Emperor's Royal Guard
- Gammorean Guard
- General Madine
- Klaatu
- Klaatu (In Skiff Guard Outfit)
- Lando Calrissian (Skiff Guard Disguise)
- Logray (Ewok Medicine Man)

Luke Skywalker (Jedi Knight Outfit) [green lightsaber variation], 1983, **$375-$425+ MOC** [POTF packaging]; **$32-$42+ MLC** ["snap" cape & green saber]. Luke Skywalker (Jedi Knight Outfit) is not only one of the most beautifully designed vintage *Star Wars* figures, but is a toy possessing myriad variations that impact its value. From two different color lightsabers (green = common, blue = uncommon), to variations in the shades and molds of his Palace Blaster, and even differences—subtle and otherwise—in his Jedi robe (the rarest version has a snap in place of a permanent stitch), this figure is in very high demand. Here, the character is displayed on his rarest packaging variant: the vintage Power of the Force assortment with Collector Coin. What follows is the pricing for "Luke Jedi," ROTJ packaging: **$190-$225+ MOC** [blue saber]; **$100-$120+ MOC** [green saber]; **$65-$78+ MLC** ["snap" cape & blue saber]; **$45-$52+ MLC** [standard cape & blue saber]; **$25-$34+ MLC** [standard cape & green saber].

- Luke Skywalker (Jedi Knight Outfit) (green [common] or blue [uncommon] lightsaber variations)
- Nien Nunb (mailer box or MOC)
- Nikto
- Princess Leia Organa (Boushh Disguise)
- Rebel Commando
- Ree-Yees
- Squid Head
- Weequay

» **1984—77, 79-BACK CARDS**

- AT-ST Driver
- B-wing Pilot
- Han Solo (In Trench Coat) (two coat variations)
- Princess Leia Organa (In Combat Poncho)
- Pruneface
- Rancor Keeper
- Teebo
- The Emperor (mailer box or MOC)
- Wicket W. Warrick

8D8 (aka. Ate-dee-ate), 1983, **$65-$75 MOC** [crystal clear bubble]; **$30-$35** [yellowed bubble]; **$5-$10 MLC**. Like many of the lesser-known characters from *ROTJ* (8D8 worked in conjunction with supervisor/interrogator droid EV-9D9 [1985] in the lower levels of Jabba's dungeon[s]), 8D8 can be found easily in his original packaging. However, some Kenner carded figures from the *ROTJ* assortment actually sell for less money (!) than their modern, updated counterparts in Hasbro's blazing-hot The Vintage Collection (2010-2013) sub-line.

Carrying Cases
- C-3PO Collector's Case [holds 40 figures]
- Chewbacca Bandolier Strap
- Darth Vader Collectors Case (ROTJ packaging)
- Laser Rifle Carry Case
- Return of the Jedi [vinyl] Mini-Figures Collector's Case [holds 24 figures]

Creatures
- Rancor Monster

Mini-Rigs & Accessories
- AST-5 Vehicle
- Desert Sail Skiff
- Endor Forest Ranger
- Ewok Assault Catapult
- Ewok Combat Glider
- ISP-6

Squid Head, 1983, **$48-$62+ MOC**; **$10-$14 MLC**.
Although many characters introduced in *Return of the Jedi* were uniquely constructed and possessed alien physiology, it was Kenner's translation of them into action figure form that truly cemented their personalities into the collective consciousness of an entire generation of consumers. Squid Head (aka. Tessek), a Quarren accountant working for the Hutt crime lord, is no exception thanks to a brilliant body and head sculpt, a magnificent soft good cape* (and skirt), and great poseability.

*NOTE: Any burgundy-cape variations of Squid Head were never released at retail in the U.S., and were solicited via Mexico's Lili Ledy line, and so were only available through the Central American marketplace. Furthermore, like any other high-end loose action figure specimens (vinyl-caped Jawas [I was scammed by this myself], "double telescoping" lightsabers, etc.), please have your burgundy-caped Squid Head checked by an authority to determine its authenticity!

Playsets
- Ewok Village Action Playset
- Jabba the Hutt Action Playset (with Salacious Crumb)
- Jabba the Hutt Dungeon (with Amanaman, Barada and EV-9D9) (Sears exclusive)*
- Jabba the Hutt Dungeon (with 8-D8, Klaatu and Nitko) (Sears exclusive)

*Note: Even though this playset came with characters released in the POTF line (1984-1985), it is still considered part of the *ROTJ* line.

Vehicles/Accessories
- B-wing Fighter
- "Battle-Damaged" Imperial TIE Fighter
- Imperial Shuttle
- Speeder Bike Vehicle
- Y-wing Fighter

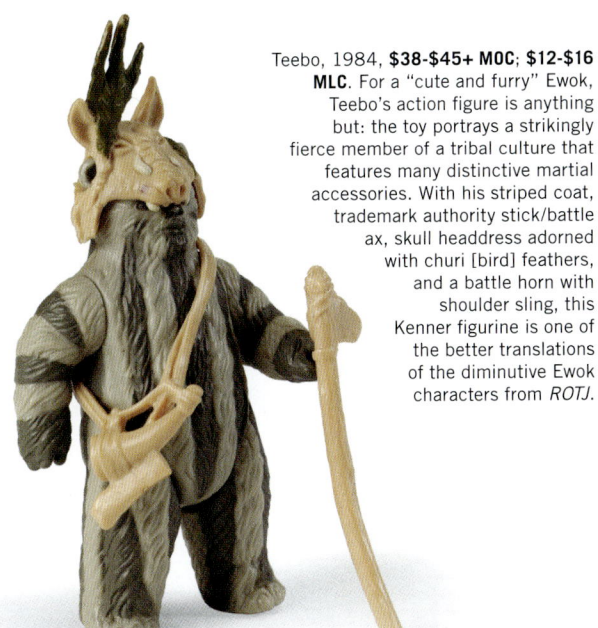

Teebo, 1984, **$38-$45+ MOC; $12-$16 MLC**. For a "cute and furry" Ewok, Teebo's action figure is anything but: the toy portrays a strikingly fierce member of a tribal culture that features many distinctive martial accessories. With his striped coat, trademark authority stick/battle ax, skull headdress adorned with churi [bird] feathers, and a battle horn with shoulder sling, this Kenner figurine is one of the better translations of the diminutive Ewok characters from *ROTJ*.

Rancor Keeper, 1984, **$22-$30+ MOC**; **$10-$12 MLC**. This action figure's appellation, Rancor Keeper, is actually Malakili's chosen vocation: the husky, empathic, bare-chested animal trainer cares after the Rancor Monster (1984) for Jabba the Hutt. One of the most common vintage *Star Wars* figures to find packaged, Kenner's Rancor Keeper action figure includes a removable hood and modified gaderffii ("gaffi") stick—which was gifted to him by a tribe of Tusken Raiders (see Sand People [1978]).

Rancor Monster, 1984, **$25-$35+ MLC**; boxed samples: **$245-$275+ MISB**, **$50-$65 MIB**. Kenner completely outdid themselves with the sculpting of this magnificent beast. With the ability for collectors to "open [the] Rancor Monster['s] jaw by pushing the lever on his back," and [to] "spread [its] spring loaded arms and watch them snap back into position," the creature's moveable legs and wrists afforded the Rancor the ability to hold many different action poses.

The Emperor, 1984, Kenner *Star Wars*, [*The Empire Strikes Back*], **$55-$65+ MISB** [all contents factory-sealed in mailer box]; **$24-$30 MIB** [w/ all included pieces (& sealed figure)]; **$20-$22 MIB** [w/ all included pieces (& non-sealed figure)]; **$7-$12 MLC**. Yet another in a long line of fabulous vintage mail-away *Star Wars* action figures, with 5 proof-of-purchase seals, collectors could obtain "The Emperor" (aka. Darth Sidious) from *Return of the Jedi* who was—according to promotional flavor text—the "Leader of the Imperial Forces, ruler of Darth Vader, and Supreme Master of the Dark Side of the Force." After submitting your POP's to Kenner, within 10 to 12 weeks, a small white shipping box arrived at your door which contained a *ROTJ* product catalog, and an Emperor action figure sealed within a transparent baggie with a glossy black cane accessory. Carded specimens of The Emperor sealed on a *Return of the Jedi* package garners **$48-$62 MOC**.

See-Threepio (C-3PO) Collector's Case, 1983, prices vary greatly based on condition: **$68-$85+ MISP** [with shrink-wrap intact]; **$32-$36+ MLC** [good chrome with I.D. insert, labels applied]; **$15-$22 MLC** [with or without I.D. insert, (all) labels applied]; **$42-$58+ MLC** [good chrome with I.D. insert & unapplied labels]. The vac-metallized C-3PO Collector's Case is described in its promotional material as a "life-size golden sculpting of the world's most popular droid, C-3PO," which "…holds up to 40 *Star Wars* Action Figures plus accessories and includes a pressure-sensitive label sheet"—with a hidden handle that allows you to bring the case anywhere. However, consumers should make sure that the C-3PO Collector's Case (as with any *Star Wars* collector's tote [e.g., the Darth Vader's Collector's Case, the smaller vinyl cases with trays, etc.]) is clean and that its labels are intact… and straight.

Imperial Shuttle, 1984, **$240-$265+ MIB** [working electronics]; **$160-$175+ MIB** [non-working]; **$160-$175+ MLC** [working electronics]; **$105-$120+ MLC** [non-working]; sealed samples: **$800-$835+ MISB**. Through the use of two "AA" batteries, a button could be pressed to hear "laser sounds," while a bevy of action features lured collectors to buy this most prized vehicle of the vintage *Star Wars* toy line. With an opening cockpit, two (2) adjustable wing laser cannons, a two-part boarding ramp, manual landing gear, a removable side panel, and wings that automatically move into various flying positions, the Imperial Shuttle toy captured the attention of many diehard *Star Wars* aficionados. With its tremendous size (22" tall with a 3' wingspan) and faithful translation into plastic form, this was the largest ship produced in the entire vintage *Star Wars* line.

Y-wing Fighter, 1983: **$375-$400+ MISB**; **$80-$95+ MIB** [working electronics]; **$58-$75+ MIB** [non-working]; **$58-$75+ MLC** [working electronics]; **$48-$62+ MLC** [non-working]. The Y-wing marks the only spacecraft in the vintage Kenner toy line that affords collectors this amazing opportunity to hold R2-D2 or R5-D4 in its droid socket. However, collectors should take note that the vehicle is a bit fragile, since each engine is able to be disassembled into six different parts. Possessing laser cannon motion and sound (via two [2] "C" batteries), remote landing gear[s], and bomb-dropping action, the Y-wing Fighter is on the wish list for many *Star Wars* fans, yet like every vintage vehicle, costs a pretty penny.

B-wing Fighter, 1983: **$375-$400+ MISB**; **$80-$95+ MIB** [working electronics]; **$58-$70+ MIB** [non-working]; **$55-$68+ MLC** [working electronics]; **$40-$55+ MLC** [non-working]. The revolutionary B-wing Fighter is a popular vintage spaceship toy on the secondary market, since it touts a bevy of action features: laser battle sounds (via two [2] 'AA' batteries), the ability to "turn [the] rear engine pad … to move wings into attack position," a gravity controlled cockpit that will "stay right side up no matter how the wings are rotated," an opening cockpit, and a lever that automatically raises and lowers its landing gear.

CHAPTER 4

Power of the Force

In 1984, a year after the premiere of *Return of the Jedi*, the original *Star Wars* trilogy was passing out of the collective consciousness as a slew of new toy and action figure offerings began crowding *Star Wars* product off retail shelves — such as Hasbro's *G.I. Joe: A Real American Hero* toys, changing robots known as Transformers: More Than Meets the Eye, and Mattel's Masters of the Universe — and so, *Star Wars* action figures had a last gasp in late 1984/early 1985 when Kenner produced the final magnificent assortment of the vintage line: Star Wars, Power of the Force.

Although hailed by *Star Wars* aficionados as some of the best sculpted and best designed of all the vintage action figures, due to waning interest in the line, these toys (packaged with a special silver-colored foil-embossed collector's coin) did not sell very well and were often discounted at retail. Due to their scarcity and limited availability in stores (many retailers were ordering lower numbers of *Star Wars* product by the time POTF assortments were released), their high level of detail and ornate packaging, these figures are in exceedingly high demand on the secondary market.

It should be noted that although fifteen all-new action figures were sculpted under the *Star Wars* Power of the Force banner (and one figure, the highly desirable Yak Face, was only available outside of the United States), many popular older figures (Ben Obi-Wan Kenobi, Luke Skywalker: Jedi Knight, See-Threepio [C-3PO] [with Removable Limbs], etc.) were re-released on POTF cards with newly created vac-metallized, chrome-plated POTF collector's coins. Many of these coins (and

Artoo-Detoo (R2-D2) with pop-up lightsaber, 1984, **$210-$230+ MLC** [with coin]; **$195-$205+ MLC** [without coin]; **$20-$26+** [coin itself]. Carded samples are quite expensive, bringing **$255-$280+ MOC**. This magnificent and highly-prized version of Artoo gave *Star Wars* collectors a reason to repeatedly check retail pegs for shipments of Kenner's peerless Power of the Force action figure assortment. Preserving the same aspects of the original R2-D2 that kids and collectors loved—a vacuum-metallized silver chromed dome, clicking head that rotated 360°, and pair of solid, poseable legs that made the figure stable beyond reproach—the designers at Kenner added one more stunning feature that sent consumers over the moon: a pop-up light saber that, when you turned Artoo's head from left to right, the included green lightsaber jumped upward (!).

other POTF coins that were only available as mail-aways off of the figures' package backs) are worth their weight in gold — quite literally — on the secondary market. Twenty-seven coins were available only through a Kenner mail-away offer; these are the most difficult-to-find of all POTF coins.

To capitalize on the poor sales of the POTF assortment and diminishing popularity of the *Star Wars* toy franchise, Kenner decided to tap into the emerging children's programming market by constructing two disparate toy lines with Saturday morning cartoon tie-ins: the Droids and Ewoks collections. Both toy lines continued the procedure established with Kenner's

Han Solo (In Carbonite Chamber), 1984, **$280-$325+ MOC; $135-$150+ MLC** [with coin]; **$95-$110+ MLC** [without coin]; **$15-$25+** [coin itself]. Most casual fans have not heard about the Power of the Force assortment and are surprised at the variety and types of figures that were solicited in 1984-1985—specifically, Han Solo (In Carbonite Chamber), which allows collectors to own a Han Solo figure that can be placed inside of the (semi-translucent) block itself.

Star Wars: Power of the Force assortment, packaging a foil-stamped collector's coin unique to each figure within the toy's blister card: Droids coins were minted in gold; Ewoks coins produced in bronze.

Regardless, we should never forget that Kenner sold more than 250 million total figures between 1978 and 1985.

» ACTION FIGURES

1984

- Artoo-Detoo (R2-D2) with pop-up lightsaber
- A-wing Pilot
- Han Solo (In Carbonite Chamber)
- Imperial Dignitary
- Imperial Gunner
- Luke Skywalker (Imperial Stormtrooper Outfit) (white samples are difficult to acquire)
- Lumat (sometimes considered part of the *ROTJ* line)
- Paploo (sometimes considered part of the *ROTJ* line)

Luke Skywalker (Imperial Stormtrooper Outfit) (PURE white samples are difficult to acquire), 1984, **$165-$190+ MLC** [with coin]; **$155-$175+ MLC** [without coin]; **$145-$155+ MLC** [slightly yellowed]; **$25-$40+** [coin itself]. Carded samples fetch a handsome price on the secondary market: **$410-$450 MOC** [non-yellowed bubble]; **$290-$315+ MOC** [slightly yellowed bubble]. One of the oft-demanded pieces from the vintage Kenner line on the secondary market, Luke Skywalker (Imperial Stormtrooper Outfit) is a dream figure for many casual collectors and aficionados alike.

1985

- Amanaman
- Anakin Skywalker (available via mail-away [common] or Mint On Card [quite rare])
- Barada
- EV-9D9
- Lando Calrissian (General Pilot)
- Luke Skywalker (in Battle Poncho)
- Romba
- Warok
- Yak Face*

*Yak Face was only released on a Canadian POTF card with character-specific coin, or on a European Tri-Logo card (without his POTF coin or accessory [either a palace blaster or a skiff guard style staff]). The character was <u>never</u> available carded or otherwise in the U.S.

The following list delineates older action figures (characters from earlier SW, ESB and ROTJ assortments) that were re-released during the POTF assortment in 1984 and 1985: each of these re-releases comes carded with a POTF Collectors Coin sealed on the card

EV-9D9, 1985, **$205-$235+ MOC**; **$95-$110+ MLC** [with coin]; **$80-$95+ MLC** [without coin]; **$12-$15+** [coin itself]. EV-9D9 inhabited the boiler room of Jabba's Palace, an area that was loosely dedicated to "cyborg operations"—a division that fell under this sinister torture droid's oversight. With an opening-and-closing mouth feature, this droid towers over many vintage Star Wars action figures and is in high demand.

front — these MOC figures are rare and in high demand, as are the coins included within their packages.

- AT-AT Driver (*exceedingly* rare)
- AT-ST Driver
- Biker Scout
- B-wing Pilot
- Chewbacca
- Darth Vader
- Emperor Palpatine
- Gammorean Guard
- Han Solo (in Trench Coat)
- Jawa
- Leia in Combat Poncho
- Luke Skywalker (Jedi Knight Outfit [green saber])
- Nitko (*exceedingly* rare)
- Obi-Wan Kenobi
- C-3PO [See-Threepio] (with Removable Limbs)
- Stormtrooper
- Teebo
- Wicket W. Warrick
- Yoda

» MAIL-AWAY POTF COINS *(sent randomly via post)*

- AT-AT
- Bib Fortuna/Majordomo
- Boba Fett/Bounty Hunter
- Chief Chirpa/Ewok Leader
- Star Wars/Creatures
- Star Wars/Droids
- Emperor's Royal Guard/Empire
- FX-7/Medical Droid
- Greedo/Bounty Hunter
- Han Solo/Rebel Fighter [original]
- Han Solo / Rebel Hero [Hoth]
- Hoth Stormtrooper/Empire
- Imperial Commander/Empire
- Lando Calrissian/Rebel General [original]
- Luke Skywalker/Rebel Leader [original]
- Luke Skywalker/Rebel Leader [Hoth]
- Luke Skywalker/Jedi Knight [Bespin]
- Millennium Falcon/Star Wars
- Princess Leia/Rebel Leader [original]
- Princess Leia/Boushh
- Star Wars/Sail Barge
- Star Destroyer Commander/Empire
- TIE Fighter Pilot/Empire
- Too-One Bee/Medical Droid
- Tusken Raider/Sand People
- Zuckuss/Bounty Hunter

Ewok Battle Wagon, 1985, **$650-$725+ MISB**; **$245-$265+ MIB**; **$180-$205+ MLC**; **$180-$205+ MLC**. The Ewok Battle Wagon is an impossible vehicle to find complete due to a complex assortment of esoteric parts. Solicited for the Power of the Force line but appearing on 1985's *Ewoks* sub-line as well, the Battle Wagon is a deceptively rare and intricately designed war machine. If you're looking to pick one up for your collection, please make sure to consult an online resource or hard copy guide that will ensure you will obtain every one of the vehicle's obscure accoutrements. From its Tree Branch Hook with brown string to its two (2) faux-wood "T"-cranks, Wicket the Ewok's military transport is quickly becoming one of the hardest-to-find vehicles of the vintage Kenner *Star Wars* line—growing more popular (and pricier) with each passing day.

Tatooine Skiff, 1985, **$695-$745+ MISB**; **$475-$500+ MIB**; **$285-$320+ MLC**. One of the most expensive (and delicate) collectibles offered in the vintage *Star Wars* toy line, the Tatooine Skiff possesses many special features: levers trigger the ship's rudders and retract its landing pods, while a switch activates the craft's hinged gangplank. The Skiff's two side rails also fold to simulate battle damage, and there is a storage area for the guards' force pikes and staffs. Finally, a trap door "trigger" sends an unlucky passenger plummeting over the side. This über-rare vehicle is becoming more popular and expensive over time; even loose samples sell for about **$300 each**.

» VEHICLES/BODY RIGS

- Ewok Battle Wagon
- Imperial Sniper
- One-Man Sand Skimmer
- Security Scout
- Tatooine Skiff

Star Wars: Droids (Kenner, 1985)

The *Star Wars Droids: The Adventures of R2-D2 and C-3PO* animated program recounted events that took place during the nineteen-year span between *Star Wars Episode III: Revenge of the Sith* and *Star Wars Episode IV: A New Hope*. The *Droids* cartoon (which ran from September 7, 1985-June 7, 1986 on ABC) follows the exploits of the two most popular droids in the *Star Wars* galaxy: the loquacious C-3PO and his determined companion, R2-D2, as the two robots serve a series of four different masters over the course of thirteen episodes and one television special (*The Great Heap*).

Besides C-3PO and R2-D2, the toy line translated the most prominent animated characters into plastic form, including: Thall Joben, teenager from the planet Ingo with a passion for speeder racing; Jord Dusat, Thall Joben's best friend; Kea Moll, a brave and beautiful teenager from the planet Annoo who can handle any challenge; Tig Fromm, the leader of an underworld gang of thugs and cutthroats who prey on the weak and helpless of Ingo; Sise Fromm, one of the most notorious gang leaders in the galaxy whose secret desire is to run The Empire; Kez-Iban, a lost prince who was left to wander from planet to planet after his memory was stripped by an evil vizier; Uncle Gundy, an old fortune hunter whose hard luck never discourages him from seeking the "pot of gold" on every planet; Jann Tosh, a teenager who was orphaned in the Clone Wars and now travels with the adventurous Uncle Gundy; Boba Fett, the most notorious bounty hunter in the galaxy; and the A-Wing Pilot, daring and fearless pilot of the speedy A-Wing Fighter.

Along with the twelve aforementioned action figures

C-3PO [animated design], 1985, *Droids*, **$450-$485+ MOC**; **$325-$360+ MLC** [with coin]; **$285-$310 MLC** [without coin]; **$45-$50+** [coin itself]. The rarest version of C-3PO is this *Droids* incarnation, which is the exact same toy as his second version—1982's C-3PO (with Removable Limbs)—except that instead of vac-metallized golden chrome covering Threepio's body, Kenner painted the character to match the colors he exhibited in *Star Wars Droids: The Adventures of R2-D2 and C-3PO*. And like every other carded *Droids* figure, he comes with a gold-plated Collector Coin, yet carded samples are exorbitant.

Sise Fromm, 1985, [*Droids*], **$385-$425 MOC**; **$325-$385+ MLC** [with coin]; **$275-$325+ MLC** [without coin]; **$35-$42+** [coin itself]. Characterized on his package back as "…one of the most notorious gang leaders in the galaxy whose secret desire is to run THE EMPIRE, the sinister Sise Fromm and his Fromm Gang of criminal thugs… subjugate and terrorize the inhabitants of the backwater Mid Rim world known as Ingo," specifically, R2-D2, C-3PO, and their masters Thall Joben and Jord Dusat (along with their ally, Kea Moll). As a collectible toy, the corpulent Sise Fromm possesses one lone accessory: a single, hard-to-find purple robe. Packaged samples of this figure are quite rare.

A-wing Fighter, 1985, [*Droids*], **$475-$510 MISB**; **$240-$245+ MIB** [working electronics]; **$210-$220+ MIB** [non-working]; **$165-$185+ MLC** [working electronics]; **$130-$155+ MLC** [non-working]; **$165-$185+ MLC** [working electronics]. The beautifully-designed *Droids* A-wing Fighter, with its adjustable laser cannons with battery-triggered laser sound, automatically-triggered landing gear and cockpit canopy is considered a Holy Grail for many vintage *Star Wars* collectors. Although featured in the Battle of Endor during *Episode VI*, the ship was never produced under any facet of Kenner's vintage Star Wars line, even though the ship's navigator was. The A-wing Pilot was solicited in the Power of the Force assortment—without his requisite starfighter. Boxed samples of the toy are darned expensive.

(two of which were straight re-issues of *Star Wars* figures in Droids packaging [Boba Fett, A-Wing Pilot]; two others used the same molds as their *Star Wars* counterparts, but were rendered in different paint and/or sticker schemes [C-3PO, R2-D2]). Kenner also produced three outstanding vehicles for the Droids toy line: the ATL-Interceptor, the Side Gunner, and the beautifully constructed, highly-prized, and VERY expensive A-Wing Fighter.

» ACTION FIGURES
- A-wing Pilot
- Boba Fett
- C-3PO (See-Threepio) (NOT gold-chromed — animated aesthetic, same body mold as ESB See-Threepio [with removable limbs])
- Jann Tosh
- Jord Dusat
- Kea Moll
- Kez-Iban
- R2-D2 (Artoo-Deeto) (animated aesthetic, same body mold as POTF R2-D2 [with pop-up lightsaber])
- Sise Fromm
- Thall Joben
- Tig Fromm
- Uncle Gundy

» VEHICLES
- ATL Interceptor
- A-wing Fighter
- [Imperial] Side Gunner

Star Wars: Ewoks (Kenner, 1985)

Hoping to capture the imagination of the horde of young children who worshipped the furry, quirky, cute, teddy bear-esque Ewoks — those adorable hunter-gatherers who inhabited the forest moon of Endor in *Star Wars Episode VI: Return of the Jedi* — the *Ewoks* animated series was broadcast from September 7, 1985 to December 13, 1986. The *Ewoks* cartoon revolved around the antics of Wicket W. Warrick, Princess Kneesaa, and their tribe of Ewoks as they fight against another clan,

Wicket W. Warrick [animated design], 1985, [*Ewoks*], **$125-$150+ MOC; $85-$105+ MLC** [with coin]; **$65-$85+ MLC** [without coin]; **$20-$25** [coin itself]. This animated version of Wicket W. Warrick was constructed from a clearly different sculpt than his *Return of the Jedi* counterpart; like the rest of the Ewoks and Droids characters offered in 1985, these new sculpts are meant to reflect the characters' animated origin, like every other carded Ewoks figure, he comes with a bronze-plated Collector Coin, yet carded samples are relatively difficult to obtain.

King Gorneesh, 1985, [*Ewoks*], **$45-$60+ MOC; $30-$45+ MLC** [with coin]; **$20-$24+ MLC** [without coin]; **$6-$12** [coin itself]. The character's card back described King Gorneesh as follows: "The conniving king of the Duloks who hopes to enslave the Ewoks." With his long gray Dulok Chieftain Staff and bronze EWOKS "King Gorneesh/Dulok" Collector Coin, Gorneesh is "King of the evil DULOKS who leads them in attacks on their distant cousin, the EWOKS." Demand for all Ewoks figures has risen sharply during the past two years—particularly carded samples.

the sinister Duloks — distant cousins to the Ewoks.

The Kenner Ewoks toy line was targeted for younger children, as the figures' lack of poseability and bright colors suggest. Of the two spin-off cartoons — Droids and Ewoks — the Ewoks line is least similar to the original vintage *Star Wars* action figures. Although only six characters from the cartoon were released at retail (more were planned), no vehicles or playsets accompanied these toys. Rather than engage in the costly process of repackaging older *Star Wars* vehicles and playsets under the Ewoks banner, Kenner simply re-solicited Ewok-themed toys from *Star Wars*' Power of the Force and *Return of the Jedi* assortments and offered them on Ewoks packaging; so then, the Return of the Jedi Ewok Village, Ewok Combat Glider, Ewok Assault Catapult, and the Power of the Force Ewok Battle Wagon wound up on the 1985 Ewok card back.

The six characters released as action figures for Kenner's Ewoks toy line were: Wicket W. Warrick, a friendly and inquisitive young Ewok who loves adventure; Lograv, wise old medicine man who aids the Ewoks with magic spells and potions; King Gorneesh, the conniving king of the Duloks who hopes to enslave the Ewoks; Urgah Lady Gorneesh, sly mate of King Gorneesh who aids him in his devious plans; Dulok Scout, a loathsome, villainous, swamp-dwelling creature who spies on the Ewoks; and the Dulok Shaman, an inept "witch doctor" who uses nasty tricks to attempt to frighten or outwit the Ewoks. Unfortunately, like the Droids line, many important characters were not produced (such as Morag, the Tulgah Witch) due to the short period of the toys' release.

» ACTION FIGURES

- Dulok Scout
- Dulok Shaman
- King Gorneesh
- Logray
- Urgah Lady Gorneesh
- Wicket W. Warrick

CHAPTER 5

Power of the Force II

After the absolute dearth of *Star Wars* product from the marketplace for more than a decade, the most revered action figure franchise of all time returned to retail in 1995. With Kenner Toys now absorbed as a facet of Hasbro Incorporated, the *Star Wars* line would be re-introduced under "The Power of the Force" banner, produced by Kenner/Hasbro. However, since the tail end of the vintage *Star Wars* brand had been previously released with a Power of the Force product line (ca. 1985, see Chapter 4), fans have dubbed this resurrection of the enduring franchise "Power of the Force II" (aka. "POTF II"). The line was produced through 2000.

POTF II 'Red Lightsaber' packaging (1995-1996)

POTF II action figure product was distributed *everywhere* — toy stores, department stores, grocers, and even pharmacies — particularly at the beginning of the assortment's release in 1995 and 1996 when diehard fans clamored for any and all new *Star Wars* product and simply couldn't get enough of these toys: the early POTF II assortment[s] sold like wildfire. This new *Star Wars* line provided rabid collectors with the first new assortment of figures in a decade with the release of their first series of product in late 1994/early 1995. With Darth Vader's face in profile prominently presented on the package front accompanied by the lit blade of a red lightsaber located behind the action figure and its accessories, this first assortment of new *Star Wars* figures simply flew off of the pegs. However, the toys were met with a small amount of criticism due to their highly-masculine, nearly muscle-bound proportions — an approach Hasbro took to replicate the popular characteristics of the more macho boy's toy lines of the mid-nineties such as superheroes or professional wrestlers. Regardless, the first series featured a dozen of the most prominent characters from the original trilogy, and

Bantha and Tusken Raider, 1998, Power of the Force II [*A New Hope*], **$18-$24 MLC**. One of the first all-new creature sculpts devised by Kenner/Hasbro, the Bantha with Tusken Raider featured lifelike fur ("real-feel hair") for the beast of burden, as well as a saddle and a scale that perfectly matched the 1:18 (3-3/4") scale for each Tusken Raider (Sand Person) action figure who might interact with their chosen bonded animal. These sets may sometimes sell for as much as **$40+ MIB**.

aficionados were thrilled at the new action figures who were packaged with unique, character-based accessories and the [now] industry-standard cut-out, "collect 'em all" identification card printed on the package back.

It should be further noted that there are variations of these POTF II action figures that many diehard collectors are eager to track down. From a difference in the length of blades re: those characters equipped with lightsabers (Ben [Obi-Wan] Kenobi, Darth Vader, Luke Skywalker, etc., etc.), to the far rarer (and slightly different) paint applications utilized on the hand[s] and shoulders of the Boba Fett figure, these variations are always desirable to *Star Wars* aficionados.

» ACTION FIGURES

- Ben (Obi-Wan) Kenobi with Lightsaber and Removable Cloak!
- Boba Fett with Sawed-Off Blaster Rifle and Jet Pack!
- C-3PO with Realistic Metallized Body!
- Chewbacca with Bowcaster and Heavy Blaster Rifle!
- Darth Vader with Lightsaber and Removable Cape!
- Han Solo with Heavy Assault Rifle and Blaster!
- Lando Calrissian with Heavy Rifle and Blaster Pistol!
- Luke Skywalker with Grappling-Hook Blaster and Lightsaber!
- Luke Skywalker in X-wing Fighter Pilot Gear with Lightsaber and Blaster Pistol!
- Princess Leia Organa with "Laser" Pistol and Assault Rifle!
- R2-D2 with Light-Pipe Eye Port and Retractable Leg!
- Stormtrooper with Blaster Rifle and Heavy Infantry Cannon!

The success of the dozen 1995 "red card" releases led to the injection of another 14 action figures based

R2-D2 with Light-Pipe Eye Port and Retractable Leg, 1995, **$5-$7 MOC**. For the first time ever (unless you count the R2 droid you could assemble in Kenner's Droid Factory wa-a-a-ay back in 1979), collectors could finally obtain an R2-D2 action figure with a middle leg, which makes this POTF II version of this iconic, diminutive droid exceptionally authentic.

upon other popular characters gleaned from the vintage Kenner line, toys which were updated and redesigned for 1996's POTF II assortment — where Kenner/Hasbro began to slowly eliminate the muscle-bound attributes of the first series' designs. Furthermore and for the very first time, fans were treated to receive the Empire's villainous shock trooper who was perfectly adapted for a desert environment: the Imperial Sandtrooper (essentially, a desert Stormtrooper)—appropriately sporting an SD-48 survival backpack, officer's shoulder pauldron, and DL-19 heavy blaster rifle.

» ACTION FIGURES

- Death Star Gunner with Radiation Suit and Blaster Pistol
- Greedo with Rodian Blaster Rifle
- Han Solo in Carbonite Block
- Han Solo in Hoth Gear with Blaster Pistol and Assault Rifle!
- Jawas with Glowing Eyes and Ionization Blasters
- Luke Skywalker in Dagobah Fatigues with Lightsaber and Blaster Pistol!

- Jedi Knight Luke Skywalker with Lightsaber and Removable Cloak
- Luke Skywalker in Stormtrooper Disguise with Imperial Issue Blaster
- Momaw Nadon "Hammerhead" with Double-Barreled Laser Cannon
- R5-D4 with Concealed Photon Missile Launcher
- Tatooine Stormtrooper [aka. Sandtrooper] with Concussion Grenade Cannon
- TIE Fighter Pilot with Imperial Blaster Pistol and Rifle!
- Tusken Raider with Gaderffii Stick Battle Club
- Yoda with Jedi Trainer Backpack and Gimer Stick!

» CARRY CASES
- Power of the Force Official Collector Case
- Talking C-3PO Carry Case (Electronic)

» DELUXE FIGURES
- Han Solo with Smuggler Flight Pack
- Luke Skywalker's Desert Sport Skiff
- [Crowd Control] Stormtrooper

» EXCLUSIVE FIGURES
- Han Solo in Stormtrooper Disguise (Kellogg's mail-away)

» PLAYSETS
- Death Star Escape
- Detention Block Rescue

» VEHICLES
- (Imperial) AT-ST (Scout Walker)
- Landspeeder
- Millennium Falcon (Electronic)
- Rebel Snowspeeder (Electronic)
- (Imperial) Speeder Bike with Biker Scout Stormtrooper
- TIE Fighter
- X-wing Fighter (Electronic)

Han Solo with Heavy Assault Rifle and Blaster, 1995, Power of the Force II; red card [*A New Hope*], **$3-$5 MOC**. When Kenner/Hasbro resuscitated the *Star Wars* action figure franchise in 1995 with their Power of the Force II sub-line, they sold these figures in LUDICROUS numbers—they simply couldn't keep retail pegs stocked. The famed smuggler Han Solo was one of the first characters solicited during this renaissance, but as can be clearly observed (particularly with Han and Luke Skywalker), the figures' sculpts were a bit beefy. Looking back at these action figures now makes them appear too masculine and broad-shouldered, and because of their weak sculpts, there is little demand for these action figures on the secondary market. There have been dozens of Han Solo figures released since 1995, and 98 percent of them possess better, more authentic measurements than his red-carded POTF II version. Even with its cut-out I.D. card and extra accessories, this red-carded Han Solo—like most of his red-carded counterparts from the POTF II sub-line—might sell for a mere **$3-$5 MOC**, or **$1.50-$3.50 MLC**. Sadly, this is less money than we paid for these figures at retail nearly twenty years ago.

POTF II Shadows of the Empire packaging (1996)

Furthermore, in 1996 Kenner/Hasbro also treated longtime *Star Wars* fans with a five-figure assortment of characters based upon the multimedia project created by Lucasfilm in 1996. Described as " ... a movie project without the movie" that functioned to fill the gap that existed between *Episode V* (*The Empire Strikes Back*) and *Episode VI* (*Return of the Jedi*), this brief foray into the franchise's expanded universe yielded five figures, a pair of action figure two-packs (each set bound with a Dark Horse Comic), and three interesting vehicles, one of which — Dash Rendar's Outrider — remains a magnificently designed starfighter even today.

- » ACTION FIGURES
  - Chewbacca in Bounty Hunter Disguise with Vibro Axe and Heavy Blaster Rifle
  - Dash Rendar with Heavy Weapons Pack
  - Leia in Boushh Disguise with Blaster Rifle and Bounty Hunter Helmet
  - Luke Skywalker in Imperial Guard Disguise with Taser Staff Weapon
  - Prince Xizor with Energy Blade Shields
- » FIGURE TWO-PACKS
  - Boba Fett vs. IG-88
  - Prince Xizor vs. Darth Vader
- » VEHICLES
  - Boba Fett's Slave I
  - Dash Rendar's Outrider
  - Swoop vehicle

POTF II 'Green Lightsaber' packaging (1997-1998)

In 1997, following the 20th anniversary theatrical release of *The Star Wars Trilogy Special Edition* for the original trilogy (*Episodes IV-VI*), the packaging design of POTF II toys was tweaked a bit: now *Star Wars* product was adorned with a *green* lightsaber glow instead of the once-standard red. Then, following the lightsaber color change, an even more interesting (albeit short-lived) package transition occurred: a foil hologram ("holofoil") sticker was placed atop the film photo of the character in question, adding a unique depth to the packaging. All told, 29 new figures were injected into the POTF II line in 1997, available on these new "green cards" — solicited with (later releases) or without (early releases) the holofoil sticker. Influenced by the *Special Edition* of the *Star Wars* films, much of the product in 1997 featured all-new characters added to the movies such as the ASP-7 Droid action figure and the Jawas' Ronto mount, or other popular characters who wit-

Luke Skywalker in Imperial Guard Disguise with Taser Staff Weapon, 1996, Power of the Force II, [*Shadows of the Empire*], **$5-$7 MOC**. Part of the *Star Wars* "Expanded Universe" (EU)—a term utilized to encompass "all of the officially licensed, fictional material of the *Star Wars* saga, outside of the six feature films, *The Clone Wars* film and series, and [the] *Rebels* series produced by Lucasfilm. The expanded universe includes books, comic books, video games, toys, and other assorted media." *Shadows of the Empire* was one aspect of the EU that was created to bridge the gap between Episodes V and VI. Unfortunately, in spring 2014 the Walt Disney Company announced that all previously

released Expanded Universe content would be rebranded as *Star Wars Legends*—and would not be considered part of the *Star Wars* canon. Luke Skywalker in Imperial Guard Disguise was one of the characters currently "on the outs," and as such the demand for *Shadows of the Empire* product has waned. MLC samples of this cool-looking figure fetch less than $5—and can sometimes sink as low as $2 or $3.

(Imperial) Speeder Bike with Biker Scout Stormtrooper, 1995, Power of the Force II; red lightsaber packaging [*A New Hope*], **$7-$11 MIB**. One of the preeminent "troop builders" in the entire history of the *Star Wars* universe, the Speeder Bike—with requisite Biker Scout Stormtrooper (aka. Biker Scout/Scout Trooper), the low price of this set allows super-collectors to pick up as many of these well-designed sets as possible. Originally solicited at $9.99, if they can be found at under $10 a pop shipped—the well-weathered Speeder Bike with break-apart action, and the appropriately-posed Biker Scout—you shouldn't EVER pass this one up. In loose samples, make sure that the two maneuvering controls are intact.

nessed a redesign such as the digitally-rendered Jabba the Hutt or selectively-added Patrol Dewback beast of burden — all modified in *Episode IV: A New Hope*.

» ACTION FIGURES

- 2-1B Medical Droid with Medical Diagnostic Computer
- 4-LOM with Blaster Pistol and Blaster Rifle
- Admiral Ackbar with Comlink Wrist Blaster
- ASP-7 Droid with Spaceport Supply Rods
- AT-ST Driver with Blaster Rifle and Pistol
- Bib Fortuna with Hold-Out Blaster
- Bossk with Blaster Rifle and Pistol
- Darth Vader with Lightsaber and Removable Cape! (two different sculpts)
- Dengar with Blaster Rifle
- Emperor Palpatine with Walking Stick
- Emperor's Royal Guard with Force Pike
- EV-9D9 with Datapad
- Gamorrean Guard with Vibro-Ax
- Garindan (Long Snoot) with Hold-Out Pistol
- Grand Moff Tarkin with Imperial Issue Blaster Rifle and Pistol
- Bespin Han Solo with Heavy Assault Rifle and Blaster
- Han Solo in Endor Gear with Blaster Pistol
- Hoth Rebel Soldier with Survival Backpack and Blaster Rifle
- Lando Calrissian as Skiff Guard with Skiff Guard Force Pike
- Luke Skywalker in Ceremonial Outfit with Medal of Valor and Blaster Pistol
- Luke Skywalker in Hoth Gear with Blaster Pistol and Lightsaber
- Malakili (Rancor Keeper) with Long-Handled Vibro-Blade
- Nien Nunb with Blaster Pistol and Blaster Rifle

- Ponda Baba with Blaster Pistol and Rifle
- Princess Leia Organa as Jabba's Prisoner
- Rebel Fleet Trooper with Blaster Pistol and Rifle
- Saelt-Marae (Yak Face) with Battle Staff
- Snowtrooper with Imperial Issue Blaster Rifle
- Weequay with Force Pike and Blaster Rifle

» CARRY CASES

1997
- Millennium Falcon Carry Case (with exclusive Wedge Antilles)

1998
- Millennium Falcon Carry Case (with Imperial Scanning Crew Trooper)

» CINEMA SCENES (3-PACKS)
- Cantina Showdown
  - » *(Dr. Evazan, Ponda Baba, Obi-Wan Kenobi) (Walmart exclusive)*
- Death Star Escape
  - » *(Han Solo [Stormtrooper], Chewbacca, Luke Skywalker [Stormtrooper]) (Toys"R"Us exclusive)*
- Final Jedi Duel
  - » *(Emperor Palpatine, Darth Vader, Luke Skywalker)*
- Jabba the Hutt's Dancers
  - » *(Rystáll, Greeata, Lyn Me)*
- Mynock Hunt
  - » *(Chewbacca, Princess Leia Organa, Han Solo)*
- Purchase of the Droids
  - » *(Uncle Owen Lars, C-3PO, Luke Skywalker)*

» COMPLETE GALAXY
- Dagobah with Yoda
- Death Star with Darth Vader
- Endor with Ewok
- Tatooine with Luke Skywalker

» CREATURE SETS
- Bantha and Tusken Raider

- Dewback and Sandtrooper
- Jabba the Hutt and Han Solo
- Luke Skywalker and Tauntaun
- Rancor and Luke Skywalker
- Ronto with Jawa
- Tauntaun and Han Solo
- Wampa and Luke Skywalker

» DELUXE FIGURES
- Boba Fett with Wing-Blast Rocketpack and Overhead Cannon
- Hoth Rebel Soldier with Anti-Vehicle Laser Cannon
- Probe Droid
- Snowtrooper with E-Web Heavy Repeating Blaster

» ELECTRIC POWER F/X
- Ben (Obi-Wan) Kenobi (with Glowing Lightsaber and Remote Dueling Action)
- Darth Vader (with Glowing Lightsaber and Remote Dueling Action)
- Emperor Palpatine (with Dark Side Energy Bolts and Remote Action)
- Luke Skywalker (with Glowing Lightsaber and Remote Dueling Action)
- R2-D2 (with Light-Up Radar Eye, Authentic Sounds and Remote Action)

» EXCLUSIVE FIGURES

1997
- B-omarr Monk (StarWars.com)
- Cantina Band Member (*Star Wars* Fan Club)
- Luke Skywalker Jedi Knight Theater Edition (March 14, 1997 give away at theaters [150,000 total])
- Spirit of Obi-Wan (Frito Lay mail-away)

1998
- Kabe and Muftak (StarWars.com)
- Oola and Salacious Crumb (*Star Wars* Fan Club)

- » **GUNNER STATIONS**
  - *Millennium Falcon* with Han Solo
  - Millennium Falcon with Luke Skywalker
  - TIE Fighter with Darth Vader
- » **MAX REBO BAND PAIRS**
  - Barquin D'an (with Kloo Horn) & Droopy McCool (with Chidinkalu)
  - Joh Yowza & Sy Snootles
  - Max Rebo (with Red Ball Organ) & Doda Bodonawieedo (with Slitherhorn)
- » **MILLENNIUM MINTED COINS**
  - Bespin Han Solo
  - C-3PO
  - Chewbacca
  - Emperor Palpatine
  - Luke Skywalker in Endor Gear
  - Princess Leia in Endor Gear
  - Snowtrooper
- » **MULTIPACKS**
  - Classic Edition 4-pack
    - » *(Chewbacca, Darth Vader, Han Solo, Luke Skywalker)*

TIE Fighter with Darth Vader, Gunner Station, 1998, Power of the Force II, [*A New Hope*], **$4-$7 MOC**. This TIE Fighter with Darth Vader "Gunner Station" was one of three particularly odd figure-vehicle combinations that were solicited late in the POTF II sub-line—sets which can be found very inexpensively on the secondary market.

- Walmart Collector Pack (three [3] randomly-inserted red or green MOC characters—six [6] different assortments)

» PLAYSETS
- Endor Attack
- Hoth Battle
- Mos Eisley Cantina 3-D Display Diorama (mail-away [Frito Lay/*Star Wars* Fan Club])

» PRINCESS LEIA COLLECTION (TWO-PACKS)
- Princess Leia and Han Solo [Bespin outfits]
- Princess Leia and Luke Skywalker [Medal of Honor outfits]
- R2-D2 and Princess Leia [*A New Hope*]
- Princess Leia and Wicket the Ewok [*Return of the Jedi*]

» VEHICLES
- A-wing Fighter with exclusive A-wing Pilot
- [Imperial] AT-AT Walker (Electronic) with AT-

Speeder Bike with Princess Leia Organa in Endor Gear, 1998, Power of the Force II; green lightsaber packaging [*Return of the Jedi*], **$7-$12 MIB**. Although this Speeder Bike includes a specific pilot (Princess Leia in her Rebellion togs for the forest moon of Endor), demand for Leia has remained as steady as that of the generic Imperial Scout Trooper, **$5-$8 MIB**.

AT Commander and AT-AT Driver
- Darth Vader's TIE Fighter
- [Luke's] T-16 Skyhopper
- [Luke Skywalker's Red Five] X-wing Fighter (Electronic Power F/X)
- Speeder Bike with Luke Skywalker in Endor Gear
- Speeder Bike with Princess Leia Organa in Endor Gear
- [Power Racing] Speeder Bike with Scout Trooper

POTF II 'Freeze Frame' packaging (1998)

In 1998, the POTF II packaging met yet another revision. Similar to the original 1984/85 POTF line's bonus offerings: character specific, chrome-plated collector's coins which were mounted onto the action figures' packages as an added incentive to resuscitate flagging sales toward the tail end of Kenner's vintage line. In similar fashion, the POTF II line in 1998 saw Kenner/Hasbro insert a character-specific 35mm film still (with each slide framed within a sturdy plastic mount) into the newest assortment of *Star Wars* characters—as well as figures previously solicited in 1996 & 1997. The pack-in, promotional Freeze Frame Action Slides were used to depict "Actual Movie Scenes" that you could "See and Project" with the mail-away Freeze Frame viewer.

These twenty-one new "Freeze Frame Action Slide[s]" POTF II figures proved tremendously popular with collectors, to the extent that the *Star Wars* Fan Club solicited a back-lit Freeze Frame Slide Viewer modeled after the Luke Skywalker's macrobinoculars the Rebel hero used when patrolling the ice planet Hoth, along with two exclusive slides: Luke Skywalker [Hoth Gear] and Han Solo

[Hoth Gear] (for 1 UPC symbol and $5.99). Additionally, collectors could order as many Freeze Frame Slide Display Holders as necessary for 1 UPC Proof of Purchase and $2.00 postage & handling for each. With 59 total slides available, ideally collectors would obtain five Display Holders to accumulate and protect all the available slides.

» ACTION FIGURES

- 8-D8 with Droid Branding Device
- Biggs Darklighter with Blaster Pistol
- Captain Piett with Blaster Rifle and Pistol
- Chewbacca as Boushh's Bounty with Bowcaster
- C-3PO with Realistic Metallized Body and Cargo Net ("New Pull-Apart Feature!")
- Darth Vader with Removable Helmet and Lightsaber ("With Detachable Hand!")
- Endor Rebel Soldier with Survival Backpack and Blaster Rifle
- Ewoks Wicket & Logray with Staff, Medicine Pouch, and Spear
- Ishi Tib with Blaster Rifle
- Lak Sivrak with Blaster Pistol and Vibro-Blade
- Lando Calrissian in General's Gear with Blaster Pistol
- Lobot with Blaster Pistol and Transmitter
- Bespin Luke Skywalker with Lightsaber and Blaster Pistol
- Luke Skywalker with Blast Shield Helmet and Lightsaber
- Mon Mothma with Baton
- Orrimaarko (Prune Face) with Blaster Rifle
- Princess Leia Organa with Blaster Rifle and Long-Barreled Pistol ("All New Likeness")
- Princess Leia Organa in Ewok Celebration Outfit
- R2-D2 with
  - » *Spring-Loaded, Pop-Up Scanner*
  - » *Remote-Action, Retractable Scomp Link*
  - » *Grasper Arm*

- » *Circular Saw ("With New Features")*
- Ugnaughts with Tool Kit
- Zuckuss with Heavy Assault Blaster Rifle

» ACCESSORIES
- Freeze Frame Slide Holder (*Star Wars* Fan Club mail away)
- Freeze Frame Viewer (*Star Wars* Fan Club mail away)

Solicited alongside the 21 new characters, the following twenty-nine figures were previously released characters re-sold on POTF II Freeze Frame cards with an all-new bonus film slide. Most sell for the same amounts as their earlier-released MOC counterparts ($5-10 depending upon the popularity of the character): Admiral Ackbar, AT-ST Driver, Ben Kenobi, Darth Vader, Emperor Palpatine, Emperor's Royal Guard, EV-9D9, Gammorean Guard, Garindan (Long Snoot), Grand Moff Tarkin, Han Solo, Han Solo Bespin Gear, Han Solo Carbonite Block, Han Solo Endor, Hoth Rebel Soldier, Hoth Snowtrooper, Lando Skiff Guard, Luke Skywalker Ceremonial, Luke Skywalker Stormtrooper, Malakili (Rancor Keeper), Nien Nunb, Princess Leia Organa as Jabba's Prisoner, Rebel Fleet Trooper, Saelt-Marae (Yak Face), Stormtrooper, and TIE Fighter Pilot. However, there are three relatively rare, hard-to-find re-released POTF II figures on Freeze Frame cards with film slides: Boba Fett, Sandtrooper, and the exceedingly difficult-to-find Weequay Skiff Guard.

Beyond the 21 new characters and the 29 re-released figures, six all-new figures were sold in two-packs through the *Star Wars* Fan Club in 1998 (and one set in 1999 [Leia Hoth and Pote Snitkin]; each two-pack was solicited in a small white box accompanied by a laminated, character-themed *Star Wars Insider* magazine Fan Club badge:

» EXCLUSIVE FIGURES
- AT-AT Driver with Imperial Issue Blaster (mail-away)

- Death Star Droid with Mouse Droid (mail-away)
- Death Star Trooper with Blaster Rifle (mail-away)
- Ree-Yees with Blaster Pistols (mail-away)
- Pote Snitkin with Force Pike and Blaster Pistol (mail-away)
- Princess Leia Organa in Hoth Gear with Blaster Pistol (mail-away)

POTF II 'Flashback Photo' packaging (1998-1999)

One of the final waves of product injected into the Kenner/Hasbro Power of the Force II line utilized a novel method of preparing *Star Wars* fans for the first new movie in more than twenty years. Since *The Phantom Menace* was a prequel film, with the "Flashback Photo" series the toy company provided aficionados with all-new sculpts of popular characters from the original trilogy, yet inserted a unique "flashback photo" inside the package. Therefore, in anticipation of the film, the following action figure packages contained a photograph that could be manipulated (via pull tab) to switch from an image of iconic original trilogy character to their soon-to-be-introduced *Episode I* counterpart. It was certainly a nifty gimmick. Furthermore, fans should take note of the new style of POTF packaging, here: one that changed the green lightsaber blade to a green color blast effect that was placed immediately behind the action figure in its bubble.

» ACTION FIGURES, 1998
- Ben (Obi-Wan) Kenobi with Lightsaber (photo: Alec Guinness/ Ewan McGregor)
- [Hoth] Chewbacca with Bowcaster Rifle (photo: Hoth Chewbacca/Wookiee Senator)
- Darth Vader (photo: Darth Vader/Anakin Skywalker)
- Emperor Palpatine (photo: Emperor Palpatine/ Senator Palpatine)
- Luke Skywalker (Floppy Hat) (photo: Luke

Aunt Beru with Service Droid, 1999, Power of the Force II; Flashback Photo [*A New Hope*], **$4-$8 MOC**. Coming in at the tail end of the POTF II sub-line, Aunt Beru with Service Droid exhibits one of the better sculpts of the early assortments and as such still holds some semblance of value. Plus, it's a pretty great interpretation of Luke Skywalker's favorite relative. Sadly, like the rest of the POTF II sub-line, there's little demand due to the fact that since these products have been off the market, Hasbro's design technology has grown by leaps and bounds. By 2013/2014, nearly every important character in the canon who'd been offered in the POTF II line has been replaced with an action figure that was clearly superior.

Y-wing Fighter with Unique Rebel Alliance Pilot, 1998, Power of the Force II, [*Return of the Jedi*], **$32-$45 MIB**. Hasbro has always tried to reward their loyal fans with specially-made vehicles gleaned from specific movie scenes and sprinkle them with a dash of authenticity. The Y-wing Fighter solicited in the POTF II sub-line was a fine update of the Rebellion's main fighter-bomber—the first since the original was offered in 1983. Due to its excellent design, this vehicle-and-figure set still performs well on the secondary market—while the value of many other POTF II vehicles have suffered over time.

Darth Vader with Imperial Interrogation Droid, 1999, Power of the Force II [*A New Hope*], **$7-$10 MOC**. This POTF II version of Darth Vader was one of the first action figures produced with a collectible CommTech chip, mere months before the promotion premiered in the *Episode I* (1999-2000) sub-line. When collectors utilized the chip in conjunction with a CommTech Reader, the accessory would allow each individual character to speak a small amount of film-accurate phrases.

Princess Leia Organa with Sporting Blaster, 2000, Power of the Force II [*A New Hope*], **$15-$20 MOC**. One of the finer sculpts of the entire POTF II sub-line assortment, Hasbro's Princess Leia Organa with Sporting Blaster action figure showcases Leia Organa in her original *Episode IV* gown and features soft-good clothing and a nicely-sculpted blaster. Unlike many of her POTF II compatriots, the figure still retains value on the secondary market: **$10-$14 MLC**, and **$15-$20 MOC**.

Stormtrooper with Battle Damage and Blaster Rifle Rack, 1999, Power of the Force II [*A New Hope*], **$8-$12 MOC**. Like many of the figures molded at the tail end of the POTF II assortment, the Stormtrooper with Battle Damage and Blaster Rifle Rack is a spectacularly-sculpted character—even outpacing some of the more current Stormtrooper figures in terms of cost on the secondary market. And is an aberration since (sometimes) loose samples of the figure will sell for more than carded samples—simply because in MLC samples, you can see the unique accessories as they are displayed: **$8-$12 MOC**, and **$10-$15 MOC**.

Skywalker/Anakin Skywalker)
- Princess Leia Organa (Ceremonial Gown) (photo: Princess Leia/Queen Amidala)
- R2-D2 with Launching Lightsaber (photo: R2-D2/R2-D2)
- Yoda with Boiling Pot (photo: Yoda/Yoda)

» CINEMA SCENES (3-PACKS)
- Cantina Aliens
  » *(Labria, Nabrun Leids, Takeel)*
- Jabba's Skiff Guards
  » *(Klaatu, Barada, Nikto)*
- Jedi Spirits
  » *(Anakin, Yoda, Obi-Wan)*
- Rebel Pilots
  » *(Ten Nunb, Wedge Antilles, Arvel Crynyd)*

» PLAYSETS
- Cantina at Mos Eisley 3-D Display Diorama with Unique Sandtrooper
- Jabba's Palace 3-D Display Diorama with Unique Han Solo

» ACTION FIGURES, 1999
- Anakin Skywalker with Lightsaber (photo: Anakin Skywalker/Anakin Skywalker)
- Aunt Beru with Service Droid (photo: Aunt Beru/Shmi Skywalker)
- C-3PO with Removable Arm (photo: C-3PO/C-3PO)

» VEHICLES
- Tatooine Skiff with Unique Jedi Knight Luke Skywalker with Lightsaber
- Y-wing Fighter with Unique Rebel Alliance Pilot

POTF II 'CommTech Chip' Packaging (1999-2000)

The final addition to the POTF II line incorporated

an interesting gimmick that Hasbro would continue to market with their *Episode I* action figures: the use of a CommTech Chip. Used with a CommTech Reader ("Communication Output Memory Module") that was "styled like Qui-Gon Jinn's Jedi Comlink," the concept is delineated on action figure package backs as follows: "The CommTech Reader gives *Star Wars* action figures the power to speak! The CommTech Reader used with CommTech Chips (included inside and with every *Star Wars: Episode I* basic action figure) give you the power. Simply touch each figure's CommTech Chip to the CommTech Reader to hear your figure's character speak. Some will even interact with other figures! Now the Force is with you!" Each figure came with a unique CommTech chip—which afforded collectors the ability to incorporate actual movie lines and sounds in their play and set-up. Only a select few POTF II characters were released with a CommTech chip in 1999, with a handful issued in 2000.

» ACTION FIGURES

1999

- Darth Vader with Imperial Interrogation Droid
- Greedo with Blaster
- Han Solo with Blaster Pistol & Holster
- Jawa and "Gonk" Droid
- Luke Skywalker with T-16 Skyhopper Model
- R2-D2 with "Holographic Princess Leia"
- Stormtrooper with Battle Damage and Blaster Rifle Rack

2000

- Admiral Motti with Imperial Blaster
- Princess Leia Organa with Sporting Blaster

» EXCLUSIVE FIGURES

- Wuher (*Star Wars* Fan Club)

Due to the overwhelming success of the line's

reintroduction, this run of *Star Wars* action figures was as impressive as their original 1977/78-1985 releases, and provided Hasbro the opportunity to give *Star Wars* fans new and (eventually) more accurate sculpts of figures from the Original Trilogy [*Episodes IV-VI*], along with never-before created figures based upon designs which were not pursued in the vintage line. With the addition of characters such as Biggs Darklighter, Garindan, Grand Moff Tarkin, Ishi Tib, Lak Sivrak, and many, many others, the *Star Wars* toy franchise rose from the ashes to dominate the secondary market yet again.

POTF II 'Expanded Universe' packaging (1998)

Due to the success of *Shadows of the Empire* toys and its Expanded Universe origins, Kenner/Hasbro decided to choose other select characters from the officially-licensed material that existed outside of the feature *Star Wars* films, among these sources were Dark Horse Comics, Bantam novels, and LucasArts video games. Although this material has recently (2015) been branded outside of the established *Star Wars* canon. Regardless of its relation to Disney's plans for the franchise, with pop-out packaging that became a three-dimensional play scene, this Expanded Universe subset of toys proved quite popular on the secondary market and flew off retail shelves. Furthermore, apart from the single-carded, individually solicited new characters, two (2) figures were sold as a mail-away two-pack through the *Star Wars* Fan Club, solicited in a small white box accompanied by a laminated, character-themed *Star Wars Insider* magazine Fan Club badge:

» ACTION FIGURES
- *Dark Empire* (Dark Horse Comics)
  » *Clone Emperor Palpatine*

- » *Imperial Sentinel*
- » *Luke Skywalker*
- » *Princess Leia*
- » *Darktrooper* *(mail-away)*
- » *Spacetrooper* *(mail-away)*
- *Dark Forces* (video game)
  - » *Kyle Katarn*
- *Heir to the Empire* (novel)
  - » *Grand Admiral Thrawn*
  - » *Mara Jade*

» VEHICLES
- Airspeeder with Airspeeder Pilot
- Cloud Car with Cloud Car Pilot
- Cruise Missile Trooper
- Speeder Bike with Rebel Speeder Bike Pilot

POTF II 'Episode I Sneak Preview' packaging (1998)

» ACTION FIGURE
- Mace Windu (mail-away)

» VEHICLE
- STAP with Battle Droid

POTF II 12" ACTION FIGURES: 'Collector Series' & 'Action Collection' (1996-2000)

In order to fulfill the desire of diehard collectors to own their favorite heroes of the Rebellion and villains of the Empire in a larger scale, Kenner/Hasbro decided to concoct a slew of large-sized action figures. Initially dubbed the "Collector Series" (and eventually changed into the "Action Collection" in 1997), the line succeeded in providing these aficionados detailed, well-rendered, articulated foot-tall translations of the most popular characters in the *Star Wars* canon. This series of detailed 12" (or thereabouts) action figures meshed expertly with the company's standard 3-3/4-inch releases.

1996 (Collector Series)
- [Ben] Obi-Wan Kenobi
- Chewbacca (furred)
- Darth Vader
- Han Solo
- Han Solo & Luke Skywalker in Stormtrooper Gear (K·B Toys exclusive [Limited Edition of 20,000])
- Luke Skywalker

1997 (Collector Series/Action Collection)
- Admiral Ackbar
- AT-AT Driver (Service Merchandise exclusive)
- Boba Fett
- C-3PO
- Cantina Band Members (Walmart exclusives, six in total)

Admiral Ackbar, Collector Series, 1997, Power of the Force II [*Return of the Jedi*], **$6-$10 MLC.** The Collector Series doll of Admiral Ackbar still stands as one of the finest translations of a movie character into a foot-tall plastic homunculus. Although the 12" Collector Series and Action Collection figures have traditionally lost their value over the past two decades since their release, within the past year these toys have experienced renewed interest: the average standard release commanding **$5-$15 MLC**, and **$12-$25 MIB**—depending upon the popularity of the character.

- » *Doikk Na'ts with Fizz*
- » *Figrin D'an with Kloo Horn*
- » *Ickabel with Fanfar*
- » *Nalan with Bandfill*
- » *Tech with Ommal Box*
- » *Tedn with Fanfar*
- Grand Moff Tarkin (with Interrogator Droid)
- Grand Moff Tarkin & Imperial Gunner (with Interrogator Droid) (FAO Schwarz exclusive)
- Greedo ([Action Collection] window box, no front flap)
- Greedo ([Collector Series] J.C. Penney exclusive)
- Han Solo & Tauntaun (Toys"R"Us exclusive)
- Jawa (Kmart exclusive)
- Jedi Luke Skywalker & Bib Fortuna (FAO Schwarz exclusive)
- Lando Calrissian
- Luke Skywalker in Bespin Fatigues
- Luke Skywalker in Ceremonial Gear
- Luke Skywalker in X-wing Gear
- Luke Skywalker vs. Wampa (Target exclusive)
- Princess Leia
- Obi-Wan Kenobi vs. Darth Vader (Electronic Power F/X) (J.C. Penney exclusive)
- R2-D2
- Sandtrooper [orange shoulder pauldron] (Diamond Comics exclusive)
- Stormtrooper
- TIE Fighter Pilot
- Tusken Raider
  - » *(v1 w/ Gaderffii Stick; v2 w/ Tusken Cycler's Rifle)*
- Yoda

1998 Action Collection

- AT-AT Driver
- Barquin D'an
- Boba Fett (Electronic)

12" Boba Fett (Electronic) (K·B Toys exclusive), 1998, Power of the Force II; Action Collection [*The Empire Strikes Back*], **$16-$22 MLC.** Inserting "phrases and sounds" from *The Empire Strikes Back* within their electronic Boba Fett figure appealed to fans with even the purest hearts. The figure still sells for the modest price above and **$22-$28 MIB.**

(K·B Toys exclusive)
- C-3PO and R2-D2 (Electronic) (Toys"R"Us exclusive)
- Chewbacca in Chains
- Darth Vader (Electronic)
- Emperor Palpatine
- Emperor Palpatine (Electronic) and Royal Guard (Target exclusive)
- Han Solo as Prisoner in Carbonite Block with Frozen Han Solo
- Han Solo in Hoth Gear
- Hoth 4-Pack (J.C. Penney exclusive)
  - » *AT-AT Driver*
  - » *Han Solo in Hoth Gear*
  - » *Luke Skywalker in Hoth Gear*
  - » *Snowtrooper*
- Trilogy 3-pack (K·B Toys exclusive)
  - » *Luke Skywalker in Tatooine Gear*
  - » *Princess Leia in Boushh Disguise*

» *Han Solo in Bespin Gear*
- Luke Skywalker in Hoth Gear
- Luke Skywalker in Jedi Gear
- Luke Skywalker in Stormtrooper Disguise with Dianoga Tentacle
- Obi-Wan Kenobi with Glowing Lightsaber
- Ponda Baba with Removable Arm
- Princess Leia in Hoth Gear (Service Merchandise exclusive)
- Princess Leia Organa & R2-D2 as Jabba's Prisoners (FAO Schwarz exclusive)
- R2-D2 (with Detachable Utility Arms) (Walmart exclusive)
- R5-D4 (Walmart exclusive)

Han Solo & Tauntaun, Collector Series, 1997, Power of the Force II [*The Empire Strikes Back*] (Toys"R"Us exclusive), **$18-$25 MLC; $35-$45 MIB**. Although this magnificently-designed figure originally sold for between $39.99 and $49.99 at retail, the cost has decreased. From Han Solo's authentic Hoth uniform featuring a set of removable Model TD2.3 electrobinoculars, working [faux] fur-lined hood, goggles, DL-44 heavy blaster pistol, and a host of other intricate details—as well as a tremendously large "repto-mammal" as his steed—this set is a hallmark in Hasbro's 12" Collector Series line.

- Sandtrooper with Imperial Droid
- Snowtrooper
- Wedge Antilles and Biggs Darklighter (FAO Schwarz exclusive)
- Wicket the Ewok (Walmart exclusive)
- Yoda

1999 Action Collection
- Chewbacca (over 13" tall [hard plastic])
- Han Solo with Magnetic Detonators
- Princess Leia with Chain

2000 Action Collection
- Dewback & Sandtrooper (Toys"R"Us exclusive)
- Speeder Bike with Scout Trooper (Target exclusive)

Masterpiece Editions
- Anakin Skywalker
- Aurra Sing
- C-3PO with Removable Limbs

Luke Skywalker in Bespin Fatigues, Collector Series, 1997, Power of the Force II [*The Empire Strikes Back*], **$6-$8 MLC; $8-$10 MIB**. With an eye toward detail and authenticity, the 12" Collector Series kept churning out spectacular *Star Wars* heroes—in this case, Luke Skywalker in Bespin Fatigues. Yet, like all of the rest of the Collector Series and Action Collection characters, the figure has lost its charm due to modern advances in sculpting.

CHAPTER 6

The Phantom Menace

With packaging prominently featuring Darth Maul — the frightening the visage of the mass-marketed villain of *Star Wars: Episode I* — Hasbro's product for *The Phantom Menace* (1998/99-2000) leapt off of retail shelves. Collectors and casual fans alike were lined up at department and toy stores across the country, eagerly anticipating the very first minute of the products' release during a well-organized and well-attended series of

Midnight Madness events organized by Toys"R"Us stores nationwide on Sunday, May 2, 1999.

Aficionados filled their shopping carts up to the brim with multiples of each figure—one to open and one to keep mint in package—in the hope that one day soon these toys would reap them untold rewards on the secondary market when they sold these action figures a few years down the road.

Darth Maul and Jedi Knight Qui-Gon Jinn have a lightsaber duel in Tatooine Showdown, Cinema Scenes, 1999, *Episode I* (*The Phantom Menace*), **$4-$8 MIB**. This is a Cinema Scenes set that was incredibly popular during its release, but has waned in demand decades later.

Sadly, these collectors were ... wrong. They missed the mark. By a lot. Although these toys were excellently designed and well-articulated, due to the movie's mixed reviews and dearth of dynamic characters (although folks still responded to Darth Maul), retailers found themselves stuck with a bunch of *Episode I* product by the truckload. You see, following the film's release, *Episode I* product was not selling through and any automatically arriving case refreshments were subjected to price slashing and oftentimes were relegated to discount bins with "peg warmers" (those action figures that never sell; the characters who remain hanging on retail pegs for a long time, hence "warming the pegs") such as MOST Anakin Skywalker product.

It is worth noting that these figures came complete with a CommTech chip, which — when collectors utilized a CommTech Reader — would allow each individual character to speak a small amount of film-accurate phrases. This was a unique selling point for the line (note that some late POTF II releases came with a CommTech Chip as well).

» ACTION FIGURES

1999

- Adi Gallia with Lightsaber
- Anakin Skywalker (Naboo) with Comlink Unit
- Anakin Skywalker (Naboo Pilot) with Flight Simulator
- Anakin Skywalker (Tatooine) with Backpack and Grease Gun
- Battle Droid with Blaster Rifle (four variations)
  - » *Clean [no detailed marks]*
  - » *Dirty [darkened with overall wear]*
  - » *Shot [obvious blaster damage over right breast]*
  - » *Sliced [obvious silver slice damage over right breast])*

Anakin Skywalker (Naboo Pilot) with Flight Simulator, 1999, **$4-$7 MOC**. One of the many *Episode I* action figures that remained on retail pegs well past its expiration date, this "peg warmer" suffered from lack of desirability after the movie's release due to a combination of factors. Many *Episode I* figures would suffer a similar fate, with both figures and vehicles not selling through re: retail assortments. Therefore, many of these toys hold little value on the secondary market.

- Boss Nass with Gungan Staff
- C-3PO
- Captain Panaka with Blaster Rifle and Pistol
- Captain Tarpals with Electropole
- Chancellor Valorum with Ceremonial Staff
- Darth Maul (Jedi Duel) with Double-Bladed Lightsaber
- Darth Maul (Sith Lord) with Lightsaber with Removable Blade
- Darth Maul (Tatooine) with Cloak and Lightsaber
- Darth Sidious
- Darth Sidious Holograph
- Destroyer Droid
- Gasgano with Pit Droid
- Jar Jar Binks with Gungan Battle Staff
- Ki-Adi-Mundi with Lightsaber
- Mace Windu with Lightsaber and Jedi Cloak
- Naboo Royal Guard with Blaster Pistol and Helmet
- Naboo Royal Security with Blaster Pistol and Rifle

Battle Droid with Blaster Rifle, 1999, **$4-$7 MOC**. Dirty variant [darkened with overall wear]—top left; Sliced variant [obvious silver slice damage over right breast]—top right; Clean variant [no detailed marks]—opposite page, top left; Shot variant [blaster damage over right breast]—opposite page, top right.

- Nute Gunray
- Obi-Wan Kenobi (Jedi Duel) with Lightsaber
- Obi-Wan Kenobi (Jedi Knight) with Lightsaber and Comlink
- Obi-Wan Kenobi (Naboo) with Lightsaber and Handle
- Ody Mandrell with Otoga 222 Pit Droid
- OOM-9 with Blaster and Binoculars
- Padmé Naberrie with Pod Race View Screen
- Queen Amidala (Coruscant)
- Queen Amidala (Naboo) with Blaster Pistols
- Qui-Gon Jinn (Jedi Duel) with Lightsaber
- Qui-Gon Jinn (Naboo) with Lightsaber and Handle
- R2-D2 with Booster Rockets
- Ric Olié with Helmet and Naboo Blaster
- Rune Haako
- Senator Palpatine with Senate Cam Droid

To capitalize on the concept of "troop building," Hasbro hit upon this idea when soliciting the *Episode I* sub-line by producing four different variants of their Battle Droid action figure. This allowed collectors to amass an army of Battle Droids who would exhibit one of four different variants, making them look essentially different.

- Watto with Datapad
- Yoda with Jedi Council Chair

2000

- CommTech Reader
- Destroyer Droid (Battle Damaged)
- Jar Jar Binks (Naboo Swamp) with Fish
- Pit Droids (2 pack)
- Queen Amidala (Battle) with Ascension Gun
- Qui-Gon Jinn (Jedi Master) with Lightsaber and Comlink
- R2-B1 Astromech Droid with Power Harness
- Sio Bibble with Blaster Pistol
- TC-14 Protocol Droid with Serving Tray

» ACCESSORIES/ACCESSORY SETS

- Flash Cannon (Electronic)
- Gungan Energy Ball Catapult Set (Electronic)
- Hyper-Drive Repair Kit Accessory Set

- Naboo Accessory Set
- Pod Racer Fuel Station Accessory Set
- Rappel Line Attack Accessory Set
- Sith Accessory Set
- Tatooine Accessory Set
- Tatooine Disguise Accessory Set
- Underwater Accessory Set

» CINEMA SCENES
- Mos Espa Encounter
- Tatooine Showdown
- Watto's Box

» CREATURES
- Ammo Wagon and Falumpaset
- Battle Bag (Sea Creatures)
- Battle Bag (Swamp Creatures)
- Eopie with Qui-Gon Jinn

Mos Espa Encounter, Cinema Scenes, 1999, **$4-$8 MIB**.
Cinema Scenes proved quite popular with collectors over the years as they expertly encapsulate a particular act in one of the six major *Star Wars* films. From *Episode I* to *VI*, these multi-packs still prove fairly popular—but at a reduced price. Especially where Jar Jar Binks is concerned … unfortunately, many of these Cinema Scenes are worth FAR less than they were a decade or so ago.

- Fambaa and Gungan Warrior (FAO Schwarz exclusive)
- Jabba Glob
- Jabba the Hutt with 2-Headed Announcer
- Kaadu and Jar Jar Binks
- Opee and Qui-Gon Jinn

» DELUXE FIGURES
- Darth Maul
- Obi-Wan Kenobi
- Qui-Gon Jinn

» EXCLUSIVES FIGURES
- Darth Maul Holograph (Walmart exclusive)
- Qui-Gon Jinn Holograph (Walmart exclusive)

» MULTI-PACKS
- CommTech 2-Pack (Sam's Club/Costco exclusives)
- Darth Maul with Sith Infiltrator

Watto's Box, Cinema Scenes, 1999, **$15-$20 MIB**. Once a very high-demand three-pack, the request for this Cinema Scene (of a special box where high-paying customers could watch a podrace) has declined over the years. MLC samples of the piece will only command a mere **$4-$8**.

- Final Lightsaber Duel (Darth Maul vs. Obi-Wan Kenobi)
- Figure Collector 2-Pack (Sam's Club/Costco exclusives)

» PLAYSETS & CARRY CASES
- R2-D2 Carry Case (with Destroyer Droid)
- Theed Generator Complex (with Battle Droid)
- Theed Hangar (with Qui-Gon Jinn)

» SNEAK PREVIEW FIGURES (ALSO SEE POTF II)
- Mace Windu (mail-away exclusive)
- STAP (with Battle Droid)

» VEHICLES
- Anakin Skywalker's Podracer (with Anakin Skywalker)
- Armored Scout Tank (with Battle Droid)
- [Trade Federation] Droid Fighters
- Flash Speeder
- Gungan Assault Cannon (with Jar Jar Binks)
- Gungan Scout Sub (with Obi-Wan Kenobi)
- Naboo Starfighter
- Naboo Royal Starship Blockade Cruiser/Playset (Electronic) (with red R-2 unit)
- Sebulba's Podracer (with Sebulba)
- Sith Speeder (with Darth Maul)
- Sith Attack Speeder (with Darth Maul)
- Stap (with Battle Droid)
- Trade Federation Tank

» 12" ACTION FIGURES ("ACTION COLLECTION")

1999
- Anakin Skywalker
- Battle Droid
- Darth Maul
- Darth Maul (Electronic)
- Jar Jar Binks
- Jar Jar (Electronic)

- Obi-Wan Kenobi
- Pit Droids
- Qui-Gon Jinn
- Qui-Gon Jinn (Electronic)
- R2-A6
- Watto

2000

- Anakin Skywalker (with Theed Hangar Droid)
- Battle Droid Commander
- Boss Nass
- C-3PO (Electronic)
- Chancellor Valorum and Coruscant Guard (*Star Wars* Fan Club Exclusive)
- Darth Maul with Sith Speeder (Walmart exclusive)
- Mace Windu
- Qui-Gon Jinn with Poncho
- Sebulba with Chubas
- TC-14 (K·B Toys exclusive)

» QUEEN AMIDALA COLLECTION

- Beautiful Braids Padme
- Hidden Majesty Queen Amidala
- Royal Elegance Queen Amidala
- Ultimate Hair Queen Amidala

» PORTRAIT EDITION

- Black Travel Gown
- Defense of Naboo (Queen Amidala and Qui-Gon Jinn; exclusive)
- Red Senate Gown
- Return to Naboo

CHAPTER 7

Power of the Jedi

(Note: These figures are a follow-up to the ultra-successful Star Wars: Power of the Force II [1994/95-2000] sub-line, and they extended this formidable license. The sculpting, if possible, is even better than the previous line).

With a green-tinted card front (harkening back to the "green lightsaber" and similarly colored blast effect packaging of the POTF II line), Hasbro's Power of the Jedi action figure packages featured a lightsaber-wielding, full-figured image of Obi-Wan Kenobi with an ominous portrait of Darth Vader lurking behind the charging young Jedi Knight. The action figures and other toys showcased in this sub-line, from 2000-2002, incorporated characters and vehicles from the original trilogy, the EU (Expanded Universe), and *Episode I: The Phantom Menace* ... as *Star Wars* fans held their breath in giddy anticipation of the second installment of the prequels.

Regardless, the franchise utilized the POTJ sub-line to coalesce our favorite characters under one unifying banner, selling these action figures with a "Jedi Force File" — an information and photograph-laden booklet

---

4-LOM, 12", with Concussion Rifle, 2000, Power of the Jedi; Action Collection (*The Empire Strikes Back*), **$13-$16 MLC**. The protocol droid 4-LOM functioned as a translator on the luxury liner Kuari Princess where he felt less than satisfied by the meaningless tasks he had to perform. After his programming became corrupted, the droid began to victimize the ship's passengers, incidences that led him to a life of crime. Using his BlasTech long W-90 concussion rifle, 4-LOM became a bounty hunter: one of the few called upon by Darth Vader in *The Empire Strikes Back*. His 12" POTJ action figure sells for a modest **$13-16 MLC**, or **$17-22 MISB**—less money than the toy's original retail price of $24.99 (!).

amounting to "8 info-packed pages" that delineated the [vital] statistics, skills, adventures, allies & enemies, gear, and tech for every hero and villain in the line. This assortment truly expanded the scope and breadth of the Star Wars universe, tapping into as yet unexplored aspects of the canon.

» ACTION FIGURES

2000

- Anakin Skywalker (Mechanic)
- Battle Droid (Boomer Damage)
- Battle Droid (Security)
- Ben (Obi-Wan) Kenobi (Jedi Knight)
- Boss Nass (Gungan Sacred Place)
- Chewbacca (Dejarik Champion)
- Coruscant Guard
- Darth Maul (Final Duel)
- Darth Vader (Dagobah)
- Fode and Beed (Pod Race Announcers)
- Gungan Warrior
- Han Solo (Bespin Capture)
- IG-88 (Bounty Hunter)
- Jek Porkins (X-Wing Pilot)
- K-3PO (Echo Base Protocol Droid)
- Leia Organa (General)
- Mas Amedda
- Mon Calamari (Officer)
- Obi-Wan Kenobi (Jedi)
- Plo Koon (Jedi Master)
- Qui-Gon Jinn (Mos Espa Disguise)
- R2-D2 (Naboo Escape)
- Scout Trooper (Imperial Patrol)
    - » *(clean variant)*
    - » *(dirty variant)*
- Sebulba (Boonta Eve Challenge)
- Tusken Raider (Desert Sniper)

2001

- Aurra Sing (Bounty Hunter)
- Bespin Guard (Cloud City Security)
- Chewbacca (Millennium Falcon Mechanic)
- Darth Maul (Sith Apprentice)
- Darth Vader (Emperor's Wrath)
- Ellorrs Madak (Fan's Choice Figure No. 1)
- Han Solo (Death Star Escape)
- Jar Jar Binks (Tatooine)
- Ketwol
- Lando Calrissian (Bespin Escape)
- Leia Organa (Bespin Escape)
- Luke Skywalker (X-Wing Pilot)
- Obi-Wan Kenobi (Cold Weather Gear)
- Obi-Wan Kenobi (Jedi Training Gear)
- Queen Amidala (Theed Invasion)
- Qui-Gon Jinn (Jedi Training Gear)
- R2-Q5 (Imperial Astromech Droid)
- Sabé (Queen's Decoy)
- Saesee Tiin (Jedi Master)
- Sandtrooper (Tatooine Patrol)
- Shmi Skywalker
- Tessek

Unfortunately, for reasons unknown, the following action figures were released late in 2001, and at this point in manufacturing the POTJ line, Hasbro was filtering out the "Jedi Force Files" from character packages. Hence, the following characters *do not include these information booklets.*

- Eeth Koth (Jedi Master)
- FX-7 (Medical Droid)
- Imperial Officer
- Queen Amidala (Royal Decoy)
- Rebel Trooper (*Tantive IV* Defender)
- Zutton (Snaggletooth)

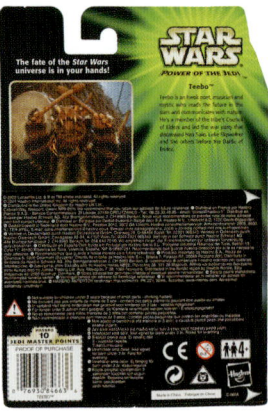

Teebo (Ewok), 2002, #040, **$6-$10 MOC**. One of the rare instances where a loose sample of a *Star Wars* action figure is worth a bit more than the figure carded and sealed within its package—because Teebo's accessories and figure sculpt are first-rate and still hold up today. This Ewok can be sold for **$9-12 MLC**.

2002

- BoShek
- R4-M9 (with added Mouse Droid)
- Teebo

» ### ATTACK OF THE CLONES: SNEAK PREVIEW FIGURES

- Clone Trooper
- Jango Fett
- R3-T7
- Zam Wesell

» ### DELUXE FIGURES

- Amanaman with Salacious Crumb (Fan's Choice Figure No. 2)
- Darth Maul with Sith Attack Droid
- Luke Skywalker in Echo Base Bacta Tank
- Princess Leia with Sail Barge Cannon

» ### 25TH "SILVER ANNIVERSARY" TWO-PACKS

- Han Solo and Chewbacca: Death Star Escape
- Luke Skywalker and Princess Leia Organa: Swing to Freedom
- Obi-Wan Kenobi and Darth Vader: Final Duel

25th "Silver Anniversary" Two-Packs, 2002: Han Solo and Chewbacca: Death Star Escape, **$7-$14 MIB**; Luke Skywalker and Princess Leia Organa: Swing to Freedom, **$7-$14 MIB**; Obi-Wan Kenobi and Darth Vader: Final Duel, **$7-$14 MIB**. For the 25th Anniversary of *Star Wars: Episode IV, A New Hope*, Hasbro released a trio of three special two-packs in their Power of the Jedi sub-line that allowed fans to "continue [their] collection with these great characters": a triad of toys that expertly captured important scenes that formulated the soul of the original film. Although the original retail for each set was $14.99, collectors can steal each of these three items at retail for the MIB prices above, or **$4-$8 MLC**.

- » **EXCLUSIVE FIGURES**
  - Boba Fett (Special Edition 300th Figure)
  - Rorworr (Wookiee Scout; from the "Invasion of Theed" adventure game)
- » **MULTI-PACKS**
  - Darth Maul & Darth Vader: Masters of the Dark Side
- » **PLAYSETS**
  - Carbon-Freezing Chamber (includes Bespin Security Guard [Star Wars Fan Club exclusive])
- » **VEHICLES**
  - B-Wing Fighter (with Sullustan Pilot [Target exclusive])
  - Imperial AT-ST & Speeder Bike (with Ewok Paploo)
  - Luke Skywalker's Snowspeeder (with Dack Ralter)
  - TIE Bomber (with Imperial Pilot) (Walmart exclusive)

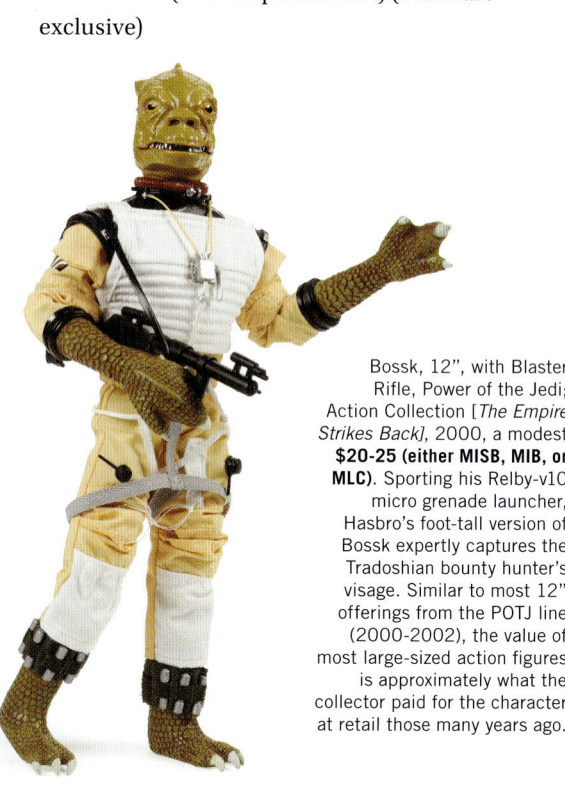

Bossk, 12", with Blaster Rifle, Power of the Jedi; Action Collection [*The Empire Strikes Back*], 2000, a modest **$20-25 (either MISB, MIB, or MLC)**. Sporting his Relby-v10 micro grenade launcher, Hasbro's foot-tall version of Bossk expertly captures the Tradoshian bounty hunter's visage. Similar to most 12" offerings from the POTJ line (2000-2002), the value of most large-sized action figures is approximately what the collector paid for the character at retail those many years ago.

- TIE Interceptor (with Unique Imperial Pilot) (Toys"R"Us exclusive)

» 12" ACTION FIGURES (ACTION COLLECTION)

2000

- 4-LOM with Concussion Rifle
- Bossk with Blaster Rifle
- IG-88 with Rifle & Imperial Blaster
- Luke Skywalker (Action Collection 100th Figure)
- Sith Lords (Darth Vader and Darth Maul)

2001

- Captain Tarpals & Kaadu (Target exclusive)
- Death Star Droid with Mouse Droid

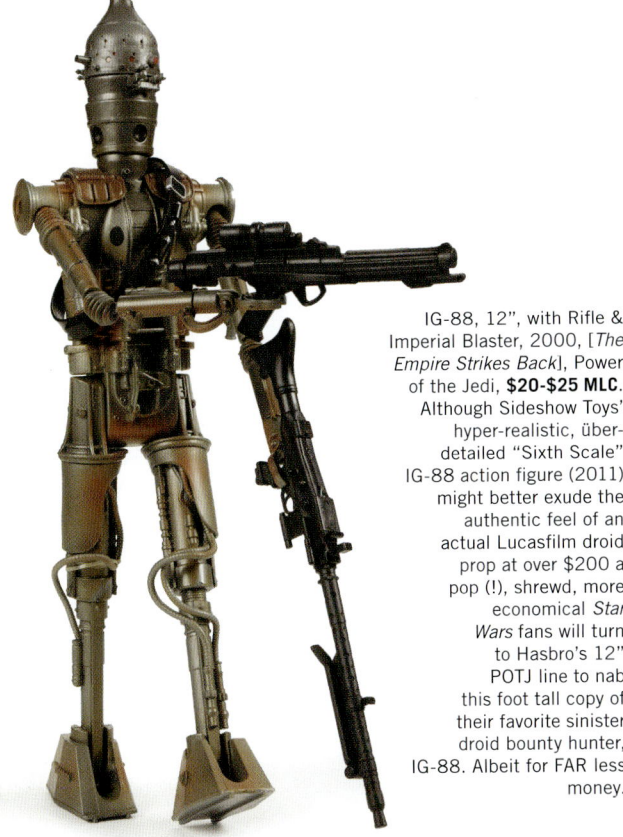

IG-88, 12", with Rifle & Imperial Blaster, 2000, [*The Empire Strikes Back*], Power of the Jedi, **$20-$25 MLC**. Although Sideshow Toys' hyper-realistic, über-detailed "Sixth Scale" IG-88 action figure (2011) might better exude the authentic feel of an actual Lucasfilm droid prop at over $200 a pop (!), shrewd, more economical *Star Wars* fans will turn to Hasbro's 12" POTJ line to nab this foot tall copy of their favorite sinister droid bounty hunter, IG-88. Albeit for FAR less money.

G2-4T, 2002, Star Tours (Disney/Fan Club Exclusive), **$5-$10 MOC**. Sold exclusively at Disney Theme Parks, the action figures offered for sale at these outlets mimicked the robots used for the parks' "Star Tours"— a way to highlight an aspect of the Star Wars universe shown exclusively by Disney. Each figure sells for roughly **$2-$5 MLC**, and **$5-$10 MOC**. However, the Starspeeder 1000 is a rare piece, commanding more than **$85+ MIB**.

- Death Star Trooper with Imperial Blaster
- Han Solo in Stormtrooper Disguise
- Luke Skywalker & Yoda (Walmart exclusive)
- Speeder Bike with Luke Skywalker (Target exclusive)

Star Wars: Star Tours (Hasbro, 2000-2002)

Solicited exclusively at Walt Disney World Resorts, "Whenever your plans call for intergalactic transport, call on STAR TOURS for state of the art travel excitement! Tour the galaxy aboard the STARSPEEDER 3000, the most advanced transport vessel of its kind, and experience the expertise of the sector's newest and most reliable Droid pilots! Reservations are limited, so book your STAR TOURS adventure today!"

» ACTION FIGURES (DISNEY/FAN CLUB EXCLUSIVE)

2002
- DL-X2
- G2-4T

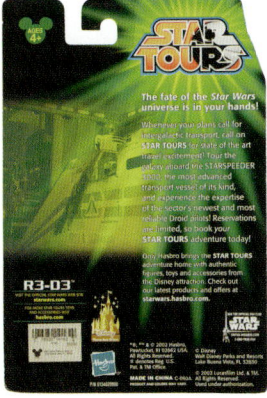

R3-D3, 2002, Star Tours (Disney/Fan Club Exclusive), **$13-$16 MOC**; **$8-$11 MLC**. This astromech droid was sold exclusively at Disney Theme Parks, and mimicked one of the robots utilized for the parks' "Star Tours" gimmick. R3-D3 is one of the most popular of these robot.

- R3-D3
- R4-M9
- RX-24 (Captain REX)
- WEG-1618

2003

- G2-9T
- R5-D2
- SK-Z38

» VEHICLES, 2003

- Starspeeder 3000

» ACTION FIGURES (DISNEY/FAN CLUB EXCLUSIVE), 2005

- 3T-RNE
- G3-5LE
- MSE-1T

» VEHICLES, 2010

- Starspeeder 1000 (Limited Edition of 10,000)

CHAPTER 8

Star Wars Saga

The *Star Wars* Saga Collection (Hasbro, 2002-2004) highlighted the new characters introduced in *Star Wars Episode II: Attack of the Clones* (which did not have its very own sub-line, but was folded into the *Star Wars* Saga) and added new additions and popular characters from the Original Trilogy and *Star Wars Episode I: The Phantom Menace*. This gave Hasbro the opportunity to appease new fans who just came on board with the new trilogy, and pacify die-hard *Star Wars* aficionados with new sculpts of old favorites. Needless to say, the line was met with rousing success.

What really made this line collector-friendly was the fact that Hasbro began numbering each new figure that was released throughout the year, and further, the company based later releases around a particular theme. Whether the adventures of these figures took place on the frozen tundra of Ice Planet Hoth, the vast and empty wastes of Tatooine, or the decadent society of Jabba's Palace—these stand as some of the finest action figures Hasbro produced.

It is worth noting that Hasbro simply called this iteration of the franchise "*Star Wars*" — it was the fans who dubbed this assortment "Saga," yet the term never once appeared on any internal or external documents.

Zuckuss, 12", with Heavy Assault Blaster Rifle, 2002, *Star Wars* Saga, [The Empire Strikes Back], **$10-$14 MLC**. The solicitation of Zuckuss in 12" form marks the final one of the six important bounty hunters who met on the deck of Darth Vader's ship, *The Executor*, to pursue the Sith Lord's hunt for the *Millennium Falcon* in *The Empire Strikes Back*. Fortunately for *Star Wars* collectors, all six characters—offered in a few different sub-lines—can be obtained relatively inexpensively.

Action Figures

2002—Note: the earliest releases of #s 1-16 came packaged with light background inserts behind the packaged figures.

- 2002-01: Anakin Skywalker (Outland Peasant Disguise)
- 2002-02: Padmé Amidala (Arena Escape)
- 2002-03: Obi-Wan Kenobi (Coruscant Chase)
- 2002-04: C-3PO (Protocol Droid)
- 2002-05: Kit Fisto (Jedi Master)
- 2002-06: Super Battle Droid
- 2002-07: Boba Fett (Kamino Escape)
- 2002-08: Tusken Raider (Female with Child)
- 2002-09: Captain Typho (Padmé's Head of Security)
- 2002-10: Shaak Ti (Jedi Master)
- 2002-11: Battle Droid (Arena Battle)
- 2002-12: Plo Koon (Arena Battle)
- 2002-13: Jango Fett (Kamino Escape)
- 2002-14: R2-D2 (Coruscant Sentry)
- 2002-15: Geonosian Warrior
- 2002-16: Dexter Jettster (Coruscant Informant)

Tusken Raider (Female with Child), 2002, #08, *Star Wars* Saga [*Attack of the Clones*], **$7-$12 MOC**, **$5-$7 MLC** (pictured); Tusken Raider (Tatooine Camp Ambush), 2003, #06, *Star Wars* Saga [*Attack of the Clones*], **$8-$13 MOC**, **$4-$6 MLC** (pictured); Tusken Raider (with Massif), 2002, #52, *Star Wars* Saga [*Attack of the Clones*], **$7-$12 MOC**, **$5-$7 MLC** (pictured). The *Star Wars* Saga (2002-2003) sub-line afforded fans the opportunity to purchase three uniquely-sculpted Tusken Raiders (Sand People). Combining these action figures with the POTF II Bantha and Tusken Raider creature set (1998), and you've greatly improved the figures' amount of playability.

Endor Rebel Soldier, unique clean-faced head sculpt, 2002, #33, *Star Wars* Saga [*Return of the Jedi*], **$5-$8 MOC** (left), **$4-$6 MLC**; Endor Rebel Soldier, unique bearded head sculpt, 2002, #33, *Star Wars* Saga [*Return of the Jedi*], **$5-$8 MOC** (right), **$4-$6 MLC**. Hasbro continued catering to collectors' needs by offering a variant for their *Star Wars* Saga Endor Rebel Solider action figure: you could purchase either a "clean-faced" or "bearded" head sculpt at retail. This was one of the first troop-builders sold with a deliberate variant and proved fairly popular back in the day.

- 2002-17: Clone Trooper
- 2002-18: Zam Wesell (Bounty Hunter)
- 2002-19: Royal Guard (Coruscant Security)
- 2002-20: Saesee Tiin (Jedi Master)
- 2002-21: Nikto (Jedi Knight)
- 2002-22: Anakin Skywalker (Hanger Duel)
- 2002-23: Yoda (Jedi Master)
- 2002-24: Jar Jar Binks (Gungan Senator)
- 2002-25: Taun We (Kamino Cloner)
- 2002-26: Luminara Unduli (Jedi Master)
- 2002-27: Count Dooku (Dark Lord)
- 2002-28: Mace Windu (Geonosian Rescue)
- 2002-29: Luke Skywalker (Bespin Duel)
- 2002-30: Darth Vader (Bespin Duel)
- 2002-31: Jango Fett (Final Battle)
- 2002-32: Qui-Gon Jinn (Naboo Battle)
- 2002-33: Endor Rebel Soldier
  - » *Unique bearded head sculpt*
  - » *Unique clean-faced head sculpt*
- 2002-34: Massif (With Geonosian Warrior)
- 2002-35: Orn Free Taa (Senator)

- 2002-36: Obi-Wan Kenobi (Jedi Starfighter Pilot)
- 2002-37: Han Solo (Endor Bunker)
- 2002-38: Chewbacca (Cloud City Capture)
- 2002-39: Supreme Chancellor Palpatine
- 2002-40: Djas Puhr (Alien Bounty Hunter)
- 2002-41: Padmé Amidala (Coruscant Attack)
- 2002-42: Darth Maul (Sith Training)
- 2002-43: Anakin Skywalker (Tatooine Attack)
- 2002-44: Ki-Adi-Mundi (Jedi Master)
- 2002-45: Ephant Mon (Jabba's Head of Security) (Fan's Choice Figure #3)
- 2002-46: Teemto Pagalies (Pod Racer)
- 2002-47: Jango Fett (*Slave 1* Pilot)
- 2002-48: Destroyer Droid (Geonosis Battle)
- 2002-49: Clone Trooper (Republic Gunship Pilot)
- 2002-50: Watto (Mos Espa Junk Dealer)
- 2002-51: Lott Dod (Neimoidian Senator)
- 2002-52: Tusken Raider (with Massif)
- 2002-53: Yoda (Jedi High Council)

Aayla Secura (Jedi Knight [Battle of Geonosis]), 2003, #11, *Star Wars* Saga [*Attack of the Clones*], **$8-$10 MOC, $5-$7 MLC**. The detail imparted onto the Jedi characters featured in *Attack of the Clones* which were released in the *Star Wars* Saga (2002-2003) sub-line was impressive: magnetized lightsaber hilts (i.e., "Force-attraction"), translucent Force effects, and detailed posing bases made these figures shined on retail pegs.

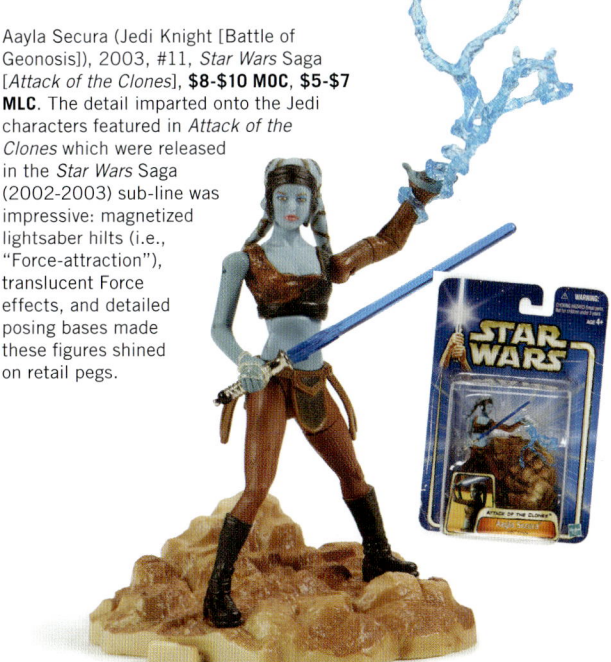

- 2002-54: Rebel Trooper (Tantive IV Defender)
- 2002-55: Imperial Officer
- 2002-56: Eeth Koth (Jedi Master)
- 2002-57: Teebo

2003

Note: It is at this point in the Saga that Hasbro made a packaging change. Following release #s 2003-07 and 2003-08, the new card backs were similar-looking but possessed a more stylish gold border running down the right side of the package. If there are two different descriptors for a particular figure, then the first is for the early card release, while the second is for the later, gold-bordered release.

- 2003-01: Obi-Wan Kenobi (Acklay Battle)
- 2003-02: Mace Windu (Arena Confrontation)
- 2003-03: Darth Tyranus (Geonosian Escape)
- 2003-04: Padmé Amidala (Droid Factory Chase) (combines with Deluxe C-3PO with Droid Factory Assembly Line AND Arena Playset)
- 2003-05: SP-4 & JN-66 (Library Droids)
- 2003-06: Tusken Raider (Tatooine Camp Ambush)
- 2003-07: Anakin Skywalker (Secret Ceremony)
- 2003-08: Boba Fett (The Pit of Carkoon)
  » *Blue color scheme*
  » *Green color scheme*
- 2003-09: R2-D2 (Droid Factory Flight)
- 2003-10: Lama Su (With Clone Child)
- 2003-11: Aayla Secura (Jedi Knight [Battle of Geonosis])
- 2003-12: Barris Offee (Luminara Unduli's Padawan [Battle of Geonosis])
- 2003-13: Han Solo (Hoth Rescue)
  » *Blue jacket*
  » *Brown jacket*
- 2003-14: Chewbacca (Mynock Hunt)
- 2003-15: Yoda & Chian (Padawan Lightsaber Training [Jedi Temple Training])
- 2003-16: Ashla & Jempa (Jedi Padawans [Jedi Temple Training])

- 2003-17: Luke Skywalker (Throne Room Duel)
- 2003-18: Darth Vader (Throne Room Duel)
- 2003-19: Snowtrooper (The Battle of Hoth)
- 2003-20: Jango Fett (Kamino Escape)
- 2003-21: C-3PO (Tatooine Ambush)
- 2003-22: Padmé Amidala (Secret Ceremony)
- 2003-23: Wat Tambor (Geonosis War Room)
- 2003-24: Coleman Trebor (Battle of Geonosis)
- 2003-25: Darth Maul (Theed Hangar Duel)
- 2003-26: Princess Leia Organa (Imperial Captive)
- 2003-27: Han Solo (Flight to Alderaan)
- 2003-28: WA-7 (Dexter's Diner)
- 2003-29: Lt. Dannl Faytonni (Coruscant Outlander Club)
- 2003-30: The Emperor (Throne Room)

Barris Offee (Luminara Unduli's Padawan [Battle of Geonosis]), 2003, #12, *Star Wars* Saga [*Attack of the Clones*], **$9-$11 MOC, $5-$7 MLC**. Once a Jedi padawan, Barriss Offee would play an interesting (albeit brief) role in *The Clone Wars* (2008-2013) animated serial as well. Take note of the development of a red-colored "lightsaber blast deflection" accessory that added play value to this sub-line.

- 2003-31: Luke Skywalker (Tatooine Encounter)
- 2003-32: Darth Vader (Death Star Clash)
- 2003-33: Bail Organa (Alderaan Senator)
- 2003-34: McQuarrie Concept Stormtrooper (Fan's Choice Figure #4)
- 2003-35: Imperial Dignitary Janus Greejatus (Death Star Procession)
- 2003-36: Padmé Amidala (Lars' Homestead)
- 2003-37: Achk Med-Beq (Coruscant Outlander Club)
- 2003-38: Ayy Vida (Outlander Nightclub Patron)
- 2003-39: Obi-Wan Kenobi (Outlander Nightclub Encounter)
- 2003-40: Elan Sleazebaggano (Outlander Nightclub Encounter)
- 2003-41: Imperial Dignitary Kren Blista-Vinee (Death Star Procession)

Please note that action figure #s 42-51 of the *Star Wars* Saga are included in the next chapter, the *Clone Wars,* a section of the canon which provided long-missing historical details of this hallowed period of time mentioned in *Episode IV: A New Hope.*

Dengar, 12", with Blaster Rifle, 2002, *Star Wars* Saga [*The Empire Strikes Back*], **$8-$12 MLC**. When it comes to selling action figures, Dengar has never been the most popular character—and the same can be said for his foot-tall, *Star Wars* Saga manifestation. Samples can be found on the secondary market relatively easily.

TIE Bomber (Walmart exclusive), 2003, *Star Wars* Saga, [*The Empire Strikes Back*], **$16-$20 MLC**. Over the course of the past thirty years, many department stores have fiercely competed over the ability to solicit exclusives: the bigger the exclusive, the most profit to be made at retail. Since this marked the very first time the Empire's TIE Bomber was ever sold, I'm sure Walmart turned a hefty profit.

General Rieekan with Hoth Tactical Screen (Hoth Evacuation), 2004, *Star Wars* Saga, Ultra Figures, [*The Empire Strikes Back*], **$7-12 MOC, $5-$7 MLC**. The end run assortments of the *Star Wars* Saga (ca. 2004) solicited some minor characters who served an important purpose in the original trilogy: among these was General Rieekan with Hoth Tactical Screen, whose appearance in *Episode V* truly begged for him to be translated into "Ultra" action figure form.

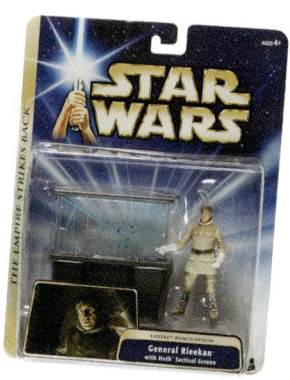

General Jan Dodonna (Battle of Yavin), 2004, #12, *Star Wars* Saga [*A New Hope*], **$10-$13 MOC**. Solicited with three Medals of Bravery accessories to place over the heads of the famous Rebel heroes after the Battle of Yavin, General Dodonna was quite popular back in 2004; his desirability continues due to the hard-to-find military decorations packaged with his figure.

2004

(SERIES 1–HOTH)
- 2004-01: Hoth Trooper (Hoth Evacuation)
- 2004-02: R-3PO (Hoth Evacuation)
- 2004-03: Luke Skywalker (Hoth Attack)

(SERIES 2—TATOOINE)
- 2004-04: Luke Skywalker (Jabba's Palace)
- 2004-05: R2-D2 (Jabba's Sail Barge)
- 2004-06: R1-G4 (Tatooine Transaction)

(SERIES 3—JABBA'S PALACE)
- 2004-07: Lando Calrissian (Jabba's Sail Barge)
- 2004-08: Rappertunie (Jabba's Palace)
- 2004-09: J'Quille (Jabba's Sail Barge)
- 2004-10: Tanus Spijek (Jabba's Sail Barge)
- 2004-11: Holographic Luke Skywalker (Jabba's Palace)

(SERIES 4—BATTLE OF YAVIN)
- 2004-12: General Jan Dodonna (Battle of Yavin)
- 2004-13: Dutch Vander: Gold Leader (Battle of Yavin)
- 2004-14: TIE Fighter Pilot (Battle of Yavin)
- 2004-15: Captain Antilles (Tantive IV Invasion) (Fan's Choice Figure #5)

(SERIES 5—STAR DESTROYER)
- 2004-16: Admiral Ozzel
- 2004-17: Dengar (Executor Meeting)
- 2004-18: Bossk (Executor Meeting)

(SERIES 6—BATTLE OF ENDOR)
- 2004-19: Han Solo (Endor Strike)
- 2004-20: General Madine (Imperial Shuttle Capture)
- 2004-21: Lando Calrissian (Death Star Attack)

» ACCESSORY SETS (ALL TARGET EXCLUSIVES)
- Arena Conflict with Battle Droid
- Death Star with Death Star Trooper
- Endor Victory with Scout Trooper
- Hoth Survival with Rebel Soldier

» CANTINA SETS
- Greedo with Cantina Bar Section

- Momaw Nadon with Cantina Bar Section
- Ponda Baba with Cantina Bar Section

» CREATURES
- Acklay (Arena Battle Beast)
- Nexu with Snapping Jaw and Attack Roar
- Reek (Arena Battle Beast)

» DELUXE FIGURES
- Anakin Skywalker with Force-Flipping Attack!
- Anakin Skywalker with Lightsaber Slashing Action!
- C-3PO with Droid Factory Assembly Line!
- Clone Trooper with Speeder Bike
- Darth Tyranus with Force-Flipping Attack! (combines with Obi-Wan Kenobi)
- Flying Geonosian with Sonic Blaster and Attack Pod!
- Jango Fett with Electronic Backpack and Snap-On Armor!
- Mace Windu with Blast-Apart Battle Droid!
- Obi-Wan Kenobi with Force-Flipping Attack! (combines with Darth Tyrannus)
- Spider Droid with Rotating Turret and Firing Cannon!
- Super Battle Droid Builder with Droid Factory Assembly Mold
- Yoda with Force Powers!

Exclusives

2002
- Commander Jorg Sacul (Rebel Pilot [George Lucas]) (Celebration II)
- Darth Vader (2002 New Toy Fair & *Star Wars* Fan Club)
- R2-D2 ([Silver Promotion] Toys"R"Us)
- Holiday [1st] Edition (R2-D2 and C-3PO) (Walmart)

2003
- Boba Fett ([Silver Promotion] Summer Convention[s]/*Star Wars* Fan Club)
- Holiday [2nd] Edition Yoda (*Star Wars* Fan Club)

2004
- Clone Trooper ([Silver Promotion] Toys"R"Us)
- Sandtrooper ([Silver Promotion] Convention[s]/*Star Wars* Fan Club)

Hall of Fame

Note: These action figures were released in 2004 on the later Saga cards: with a gold stripe prominently featured on the right side of the front (accompanied with a black Hasbro logo) box as well.

- Anakin Skywalker (Geonosis Hangar Duel)—same as Saga 2002's Anakin Skywalker (Hangar Duel)
- C-3PO (Death Star Rescue)—same as POTF II 1998's C-3PO, Millennium Minted Coin
- Chewbacca (Escape from Hoth)—same as POTJ 2000's Chewbacca (Millennium Falcon Mechanic)
- Darth Maul (Theed Hangar Duel)—same as Saga 2003's Darth Maul (Theed Hangar Duel) (derived from POTJ 2000's Darth Maul ([Masters of the Dark Side two-pack])
- Darth Vader (Death Star Clash)—same as Saga 2003's Darth Vader (Death Star Clash) (derived from POTJ 2000's Darth Vader ([Masters of the Dark Side two-pack])
- Han Solo (Flight to Alderaan)—same as Saga 2003's Han Solo (Flight to Alderaan) (derived from POTF II 1999's Han Solo [Cantina])
- Obi-Wan Kenobi (Coruscant Chase)—same as Saga 2002's Obi-Wan Kenobi (Coruscant Chase)
- Princess Leia Organa (Death Star Captive)—same as Saga 2003's Princess Leia Organa (Imperial Captive) (derived from POTF II 1998's Princess Leia Organa [All-New Likeness])

- R2-D2 (Tatooine Mission)—same as POTJ 2000's R2-D2 (Naboo Escape)
- Stormtrooper (Death Star Chase) same as Saga 2002's Stormtrooper Troop Builder Set (derived from POTF II 1999's Stormtrooper [Blaster Damage])
- Yoda (Battle of Geonosis)—same as Saga 2002's Yoda (Jedi Master)

Multi-Packs

» BATTLE OF HOTH (TOYS"R"US EXCLUSIVE)
- Chewbacca
- Luke Skywalker
- Princess Leia
- R3-A2
- Tauntaun

» IMPERIAL FORCES (TOYS"R"US EXCLUSIVE)
- AT-ST Driver
- Darth Vader
- R4-19
- Stormtrooper

» JEDI WARRIORS (TOYS"R"US EXCLUSIVE)
- Containment Field
- Fi-Ek Sirch
- Obi-Wan Kenobi
- Plo Koon
- Saesee Tiin

» LIGHTSABER ACTION PACK
- 1 lightsaber
- 3 random Saga action figures

» SKIRMISH AT CARKOON (TOYS"R"US EXCLUSIVE)
- Barada
- Han Solo
- Klaatu
- Sail Barge Cannon
- Nikto

- » **ULTIMATE BOUNTY (TOYS"R"US EXCLUSIVE)**
  - Aurra Sing
  - Boba Fett
  - Bossk
  - IG-88
  - Swoop Bike

Playsets
- Geonosis Battle Arena

Screen Scenes
- Death Star Trash Compactor
  - » *Luke Skywalker*
  - » *Han Solo*
- Death Star Trash Compactor
  - » *Chewbacca*
  - » *Princess Leia*
- Geonosian War Chamber (1 of 2)
  - » *Count Dooku*
  - » *Poggle the Lesser*
  - » *San Hill*
- Geonosian War Room (2 of 2)
  - » *Nute Gunray*
  - » *Passel Argente*
  - » *Shu Mai*
- Jedi High Council (1 of 2) [set #1 of 6]*
  - » *Even Piell*
  - » *Mace Windu*
  - » *Oppo Rancisis*
- Jedi High Council (2 of 2) [set #2 of 6]*
  - » *Depa Billaba*
  - » *Yaddle*
  - » *Yarael Poof*

Note: To review the other four components (#s 3-6) of the Jedi High Council, see the chapter titled Original Trilogy Collection (2004-2005).

Darth Vader (Throne Room Duel), 2003, #18, *Star Wars* Saga [*Return of the Jedi*], **$8-$12 MOC, $6-$8 MLC**; Luke Skywalker (Throne Room Duel), 2003, #17, *Star Wars* Saga [*Return of the Jedi*], **$6-$8 MOC, $4-$6 MLC**. At the end of the *Star Wars* Saga line, Hasbro's creativity began to shine: Luke Skywalker (Throne Room Duel) and Darth Vader (Throne Room Duel) combine to form a magnificent scene from *Return of the Jedi* that kids and collectors alike will delight in recreating.

Geonosian War Chamber (1 of 2) featuring Poggle the Lesser, Count Dooku & San Hill, 2003, *Star Wars* Saga, Screen Scenes, [*Attack of the Clones*], **$12-$18**; Geonosian War Room (2 of 2) featuring Nute Gunray, Passel Argente & Shu Mai, 2003, *Star Wars* Saga, Screen Scenes, [*Attack of the Clones*], **$12-$18**. Part of the magic of the *Star Wars* Saga sub-line was the introduction of "Screen Scenes" (a type of "Cinema Scene" that exhibited a build-a-figure concept)—where Hasbro captured certain acts within the film canon within plastic form. Although these two screen scenes were solicited separately, only upon purchasing both can they be combined to form the six figures and two table halves that yielded the full film scene on Geonosis of characters who were responsible for viewing the holographic display table in *AOTC*, prepping for the 1st battle of *The Clone Wars*.

Jango Fett's *Slave 1*, 2002, *Star Wars* Saga [*Attack of the Clones*], **$25-$32 MIB**; **$20-$24 MLC**. With an entirely new design that was noticeably different from his son's ship—Boba Fett's *Slave I* (1995), Jango Fett's *Slave I* was an incredibly popular ship with collectors— so much so that its reputation transcended *AOTC*: it would be redesigned and re-solicited many times, most notably simply as *Slave 1*, while being sold under *The Clone Wars/Shadow of Dark Side* banner in 2010-2011 in the Ultimate Battle Pack: The Rise of Boba Fett (Toys"R"Us exclusive). Regardless, with its launching missiles, sonic charges, and battle-damaged panel, this vehicle has retained its demand over time.

Troop Builder Sets
(Star Wars Fan Club exclusives)
- Endor Soldiers Troop Builder Set (4x figures—same as POTF II 1998's Endor Rebel Soldier [Freeze Frame] with minor paint differences)
- Rebel Trooper Builder Set (4x figures—same as POTJ 2001's Rebel Trooper [*Tantive IV* Defender])
- Sandtroopers Troop Builder Set (4x figures—same as POTJ 2001's Sandtrooper [Tatooine Patrol], except with clean armor)
    - » *1 enlisted trooper (black pauldron)*
    - » *1 squad leader (orange pauldron)*
    - » *1 sergeant (white pauldron)*
    - » *1 sandtrooper (gray pauldron)*
- Stormtroopers Troop Builder Set (4x figures—same as POTF II 1999's Stormtrooper [with Blaster Damage])

» VEHICLES
(*ATTACK OF THE CLONES*)
- Anakin Skywalker's Speeder
- Anakin Skywalker's Swoop Bike
- Darth Tyranus's Geonosian Speeder Bike
- Obi-Wan Kenobi's Jedi Starfighter
- Obi-Wan Kenobi's Jedi Starfighter (with Obi-Wan Kenobi) (K·B Toys exclusive)
- Republic Gunship
- Jango Fett's *Slave I*
- Zam Wesell's Speeder

(*ORIGINAL TRILOGY*)
- A-wing Fighter (with Pilot)
- Imperial Shuttle (FAO Schwarz exclusive)
- Luke Skywalker and Landspeeder
- Luke Skywalker's X-wing Fighter
- Red Leader's X-wing Fighter (Death Star Trench)
- TIE Bomber
- TIE Fighter (Imperial Dogfight)

- » ULTRA FIGURES
  - C-3PO (Tatooine Encounter)
  - Ewok with Attack Glider (Assault on Endor)
  - General Rieekan (Hoth Evacuation)
  - Jabba's Palace Court Denizens
    - » *B'omarr Monk*
    - » *Bubo*
    - » *Wol Cabasshite*
  - Jabba the Hutt (Jabba's Palace)
  - Jango Fett (Kamino Showdown) (combines with Obi-Wan Kenobi [Kamino Showdown])
  - Obi-Wan Kenobi (Kamino Showdown)! (combines with Jango Fett [Kamino Showdown])
  - Wampa (Hoth Attack)

12" Action Figures ("Collector Series")

2002

(ATTACK OF THE CLONES)

- Anakin Skywalker
- Clone Commander (yellow highlights; K·B exclusive)
- Clone Trooper
- Clone Trooper (Captain: red highlights; K·B exclusive)
- Count Dooku
- Jango Fett (Electronic Battling [with Lights and Sounds!])
- Jango Fett with Missile-Launching Backpack (deluxe)
- Ki-Adi-Mundi (Jedi Council; *Star Wars* Fan Club exclusive)
- Mace Windu (Jedi Council; Toys"R"Us exclusive)
- Obi-Wan Kenobi

- Obi-Wan Kenobi (Electronic Battling)
- Plo Koon (Jedi Council)
- Super Battle Droid
- Zam Wesell

(*THE EMPIRE STRIKES BACK*)
- Dengar
- Imperial Officer
- Luke Skywalker & Tauntaun (Toys"R"Us exclusive)
- Zuckuss

(*RETURN OF THE JEDI*)
- AT-ST Driver
- Gamorrean Guard (K·B exclusive)
- Princess Leia in Boushh Disguise & Han Solo in Carbonite [Block]
- Princess Leia on Speeder Bike (Target exclusive)

2003

(*ATTACK OF THE CLONES*)
- Anakin Skywalker (Slashing Lightsaber Action)
- Geonosian Warrior
- Padmé Amidala
- Yoda (with hoverchair & accessories)

(*RETURN OF THE JEDI*)
- Biker Scout (Battle of Endor)
- Ewok 2-pack (Keoulkeech & Lograj)
- Lando Calrissian (Skiff Disguise)
- Luke Skywalker, Jedi Knight (Slashing Lightsaber Action)

(*STAR WARS*)
- Ben (Obi-Wan) Kenobi (Tatooine Encounter [new face sculpt])
- Garindan (Mos Eisley Cantina)
- Han Solo (new face sculpt)
- Jawas (Tatooine Scavengers [two-pack])

CHAPTER 9

Clone Wars

For this sub-line, Lucasfilm's premiere attempt at rendering the narrative for the oft-referenced, enigmatic *Clone Wars* conflict, Hasbro expertly translated Cartoon Network's 2003 animated micro-series into action figure form, from 2003-2005. Consisting of three seasons and twenty-five total episodes, *Clone Wars* was conceived via the enduring vision of Russian-born animator Genndy Tartakovsky—creator of the award-winning, iconic cartoon programs *Dexter's Laboratory* (1996-1999; 2001-2003) and *Samurai Jack* (2001-2004). Utilizing Tartakovsky's inimitable cinematic style which combined elements of the *Star Wars* films with the sensibility of Kurosawa, all filtered it through a heady dose of anime.

Action Figures

- » 2003, (SERIES 1)
  - Anakin Skywalker
  - Asajj Ventress
  - Mace Windu
  - Obi-Wan Kenobi
- » (SERIES 2)
  - Clone Trooper
  - Count Dooku
  - Durge
  - Yoda
- » 2005 (SERIES 3)
  - ARC Trooper

Anakin Skywalker, 2003, *Clone Wars* [Animated] [*Clone Wars*], **$5-$8 MOC**. Based on the award-winning Tartakovsky-created *Clone Wars* animated series from 2003, these figures were concocted to mimic the feel of the animated series. Unfortunately, because of this reason, they are less than popular on the secondary market.

- Anakin Skywalker (Battle Damage)
- Clone Trooper Captain (red)
- Clone Trooper Commander (yellow)
- Clone Trooper Lieutenant (blue)
- General Grievous

» MULTI-PACKS
- Jedi Force Pack Commemorative DVD Collection* (Walmart exclusive)
  » *ARC Trooper*
  » *Anakin Skywalker*
  » *Obi-Wan Kenobi*
- Sith Attack Pack Commemorative DVD Collection* (Walmart exclusive)
  » *Asajj Ventress*
  » *Durge*
  » *General Grievous*
- Commemorative DVD Collection* (Walmart exclusive)
  » *Anakin Skywalker [new toy tooling (head, torso)]*
  » *Clone Trooper [new toy tooling (forearms, head)]*
  » *Saesee Tiin [new toy tooling (head, torso)]*
- Commemorative DVD Collection* (Walmart exclusive)
  » *Clone Commander Cody [new toy tooling (backpack, belt, head)]*
  » *General Grievous [repaint]*
  » *Obi-Wan Kenobi [new toy tooling (head)]*
- Commemorative DVD Collection* (Walmart exclusive)
  » *Clone Commander Cody*
  » *General Grievous*
  » *Obi-Wan Kenobi*

Note: Oddly enough, a DVD is not included with the above mentioned sets.

Star Wars, Clone Wars [Standard] (Hasbro, 2003-2005)

Taking place after the conclusion of *Episode II: Attack of the Clones* and before the opening flourishes of *Episode III: Revenge of the Sith*, the fascinating era of the *Star Wars* franchise known as the *Clone Wars* delineates a multimedia adventure as developed by Lucasfilm, Ltd. that pitted the Army of the Republic — the noble Jedi Knights and their dutiful Clone Troopers — against the sinister Separatists and their Droid Army led by General Grievous.

Mace Windu, 2003, *Clone Wars* [Animated], **$5-$8 MOC; $3-$5 MLC**. Due to the popularity of the later series, *The Clone Wars*, the figures based upon the animated series have decreased in demand.

Note: The numbering indicated below is continued from the Star Wars Saga (2003) line.

» ACTION FIGURES (NUMBERING CONTINUED FROM STAR WARS SAGA [#41 +])

- 2003-42: Anakin Skywalker
- 2003-43: ARC Trooper
- 2003-44: Yoda
- 2003-45: Obi-Wan Kenobi (General of the Republic Army)
- 2003-46: Durge (Commander of the Separatist Forces)
- 2003-47: Asajj Ventress (Sith Apprentice)
- 2003-48: Mace Windu (General of the Republic Army)
- 2003-49: Kit Fisto
- 2003-50: Clone Trooper
- 2003-51: Saesee Tiin

» DELUXE FIGURES

- Clone Trooper with Speeder Bike
- Durge with Swoop
- Spider Droid

» MULTI-PACKS

- Anakin Skywalker & Clone Lieutenant (value-pack)
- ARC Trooper & Clone Trooper (value-pack)
- Clone Trooper Army (NOTE: this set of 3 figures derives from 4 different molds; one figure is delineated as an officer [green = sergeant, blue = lieutenant, red = captain, yellow = commander])
  - » *Clone Trooper, kneeling*
  - » *Clone Trooper, firing right*
  - » *Clone Trooper with macrobinoculars (or Clone Trooper firing left)*
- Destroyer Droid Battle Launcher
  - » *Battle Action Destroyer Droid*
  - » *Battle Ready Destroyer Droid*

- Droid Army (3-pack)
  - *Battle Droid (red-colored)*
  - *Destroyer Droid*
  - *Super Battle Droid*
- Jedi Knight Army (3-pack)
  - *Human Jedi Knight*
  - *Rodian Jedi Knight*
  - *Twi'lek Jedi Knight*
- Yoda and Clone Commander (value-pack)

» VEHICLES

- Anakin Skywalker's Jedi Starfighter (*Azure Angel*)
- Armored Assault Tank (AAT)
- Command Gunship
- Geonosian Starfighter (with Geonosian Pilot)
- Hailfire Droid
- Jedi Starfighter (blue-and-white)

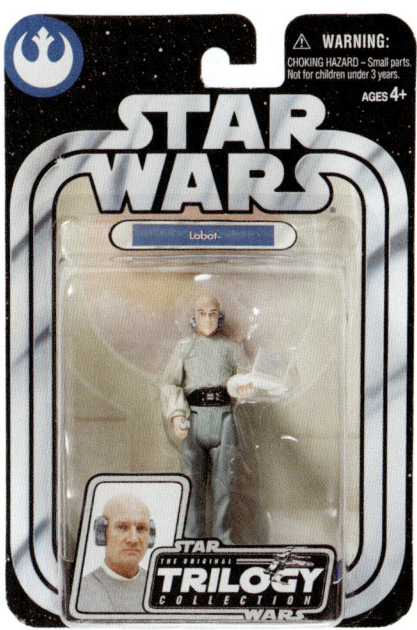

Lobot, #20, 2004, Original Trilogy Collection [*The Empire Strikes Back*], **$8-$11 MOC**. With spectacular accessories, this version of Lobot is an iconic representation of one of Cloud City's oddest (and most loyal) inhabitants.

CHAPTER 10

Original Trilogy Collection

In anticipation of the third prequel film and to celebrate Lucasfilm's autumn release of the *Star Wars Trilogy* on DVD, Hasbro solicited product from 2004-2005 based upon the first iconic *Star Wars* movie trilogy. Dubbed the "Original Trilogy Collection," this sub-line of product expertly captured the iconic characters, vehicles, and film scenes that enthralled audiences in the late 1970s and early 1980s — an excellent way to stall for time before the release of *Revenge of the Sith*. After the recent releases of

Yoda, 2004, [Vintage] Original Trilogy Collection [*The Empire Strikes Back*], **$18-$22 MOC, $6-$8 MLC**. One of the finer releases in the Original Trilogy Collection's Vintage-style figure assortment, this version of Yoda—while functioning as an homage to the Jedi Master's Kenner release in 1980—possesses enough articulation, detailed accessories, and excellent aesthetics for it to hold its popularity until the present day.

140 PICKER'S POCKET GUIDE: **STAR WARS TOYS**

product focusing on the *Clone Wars* cartoon (2003, both animated and standard sculpts) and *Attack of the Clones* related items (in *Star Wars* Saga, 2002-2003), this branch of the toy franchise allowed fans of the new trilogy to discover the first trio of films, while it also rewarded longtime fans of the brand — those stalwart devotees of *Episodes IV-VI*. With The Original Trilogy Collection, Hasbro fashioned some of the finest toy translations of key aspects of the magical *Star Wars* universe.

Action Figures

2004

- OTC-01: Luke Skywalker (Dagobah Training) (handstand or standing upright)
- OTC-02: Yoda (Dagobah Training)
- OTC-03: Spirit Obi-Wan (Dagobah Training)
- OTC-04: R2-D2 (Dagobah Training)
- OTC-05: Luke Skywalker (X-Wing Pilot)
- OTC-06: Luke Skywalker (Jedi Knight)
- OTC-07: Han Solo
- OTC-08: Chewbacca
- OTC-09: Princess Leia
- OTC-10: Darth Vader (Throne Room)
- OTC-11: Scout Trooper
- OTC-12: R2-D2
- OTC-13: C-3PO
- OTC-14: Boba Fett
- OTC-15: Obi-Wan Kenobi
- OTC-16: Stormtrooper
- OTC-17: Wicket
- OTC-18: Princess Leia (Cloud City)
- OTC-19: Cloud Car Pilot

Cloud Car Pilot, #19, 2004, Original Trilogy Collection [*The Empire Strikes Back*], **$8-$11 MOC**. The Original Trilogy Collection produced figures, vehicles, weapons, and accessories based upon *Episodes IV-VI*, and as such offered collectors newly-revised sculpts of some of the most popular characters in the canon. For instance, the OTC version of the Cloud Car Pilot showed aficionados the original, unique concept design as rendered by *ESB* designer Nilo Rodis Jamero for the very first time. That's one of the reasons this toy still retains its value.

- OTC-20: Lobot (Cloud City)
- OTC-21: TIE Fighter Pilot
- OTC-22: Greedo
- OTC-23: Tusken Raider
- OTC-24: Jawas
- OTC-25: Snowtrooper
- OTC-26: Luke Skywalker (Bespin Gear)
- OTC-27: IG-88
- OTC-28: Bossk
- OTC-29: Darth Vader (Hoth)
- OTC-30: Gamorrean Guard
- OTC-31: Bib Fortuna
- OTC-32: Lando Calrissian (Skiff Guard)
- OTC-33: Princess Leia (Sail Barge)
- OTC-34: Darth Vader (Death Star)
- OTC-35: Han Solo (AT-ST Driver)
- OTC-36: General Madine
- OTC-37: Lando Calrissian (General)
- OTC-38: Imperial Trooper

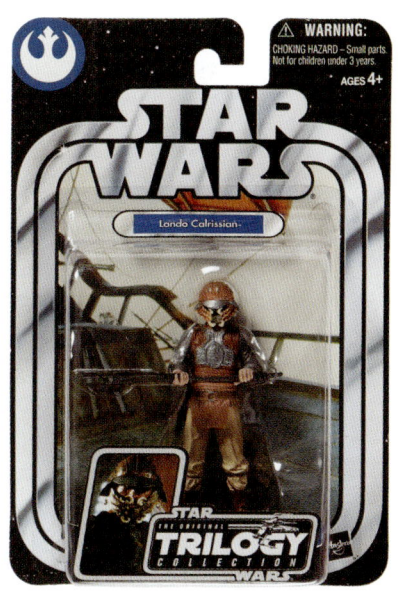

Lando Calrissian (Skiff Guard), #32, 2004, Original Trilogy Collection [*Return of the Jedi*], **$6-$9 MOC**. Still a remarkable sculpt even though it's more than ten years old, this manifestation of Lando Calrissian as Skiff Guard Tamtel Skreej exhibits one of the best selections from the Original Trilogy Collection.

Imperial Trooper, #38, 2004, Original Trilogy Collection [*A New Hope*], **$6-$9 MOC**. Snatched up like wildfire when he was originally released on retail pegs in 2004, this Imperial [Scanning] Trooper (first included with 1998's POTF II *Millennium Falcon* Carrying Case) allowed collectors to troop-build non-armored Imperial Troopers to their heart's desire.

» 2005 (SERIES 1—CORUSCANT)
- 2005-01: Pablo-Jill (Geonosis Arena)
- 2005-02: Yarua (Coruscant Senate)
- 2005-03: Sly Moore (Coruscant Senate)

» (SERIES 2—NABOO)
- 2005-04: Queen Amidala (Celebration Ceremony)
- 2005-05: Rabé (Queen's Chambers)

» (SERIES 3—CANTINA)
- 2005-06: Feltipern Trevagg (Cantina)
- 2005-07: Myo (Cantina)
- 2005-08: Dannik Jerriko (Cantina Encounter)

» (REPACKS)
- 2005-09: Luke Skywalker (Dagobah Training)
- 2005-10: Darth Vader (Death Star Hangar)
- 2005-11: Stormtrooper (Death Star Attack)
- 2005-12: Sandtrooper (Tatooine Search)
- 2005-13: Scout Trooper (Endor Raid)
- 2005-14: Han Solo (Mos Eisley Escape)
- 2005-15: Chewbacca (Hoth Escape)
- 2005-16: Yoda (Dagobah Training)

» CARRY CASES
- C-3PO carry case (Walmart exclusive)
- Darth Vader carry case (Walmart exclusive)

Exclusives

2004

- Darth Vader ([Silver Edition] Toys"R"Us)
- Emperor Palpatine (*Executor* Transmission; *Star Wars* Fan Club)
- Jawas, Holiday Edition (Holiday 2004 Edition; Entertainment Earth)
- Scout Trooper (*Star Wars: Battlefront* video game pre-order)

2005

- Darth Vader (with Meditation Chamber) (Special Edition, 500th Figure)
- Darth Vader, Holiday (Holiday 2004 Edition; S*tar Wars* Fan Club)
- Holographic Princess Leia (2005 San Diego Comic Con)
- Wedge Antilles (Internet vendors)

» MULTI-PACKS
- Clone Trooper Troop Builder 4-Pack (4 different sets: Entertainment Earth exclusive)
  » *Set #1 [white Clone Troopers, clean armor]*
  » *Set #2 [white Clone Troopers, battle-damaged armor]*
  » *Set #3 [colored Clone Troopers, clean armor]*
  » *Set #4 [colored Clone Troopers, battle-damaged armor]*

» COMMEMORATIVE TRILOGY COLLECTION* STAR WARS: A NEW HOPE (WALMART EXCLUSIVE)
- C-3PO (same as POTF II 1999's C-3PO [Removable Arm])
- Luke Skywalker (same as Saga 2003's Hall of Fame #31—Luke Skywalker [Tatooine Encounter])
- Obi-Wan Kenobi (same as POTJ 2000's Ben [Obi-Wan] Kenobi [Jedi Knight])
- R2-D2 (same as POTF II's R2-D2)

- » **COMMEMORATIVE TRILOGY DVD COLLECTION* STAR WARS: THE EMPIRE STRIKES BACK (WALMART EXCLUSIVE)**
  - » *Chewbacca (same as POTJ's 2001 Chewbacca [Millennium Falcon Mechanic])*
  - » *Han Solo (same as POTJ 2000's Han Solo [Bespin Capture])*
  - » *Princess Leia (same as POTJ 2001's Leia Organa [Bespin Escape])*
- » **COMMEMORATIVE TRILOGY DVD COLLECTION* STAR WARS: RETURN OF THE JEDI (WALMART EXCLUSIVE)**
  - » *Darth Vader (same as Saga 2003's Darth Vader from Imperial Forces multi-pack)*
  - » *Emperor Palpatine (same as Saga 2003's #30—The Emperor [Throne Room])*
  - » *Stormtrooper (same as POTF II 1999's Stormtrooper [with Blaster Damage])*

  *Note: These three multi-packs do not include a Star Wars DVD.

- » **ENDOR AMBUSH (TOYS"R"US EXCLUSIVE)**
  - » *Biker Scout (same as POTF II 1995's Biker Scout Stormtrooper from [Imperial] Speeder Bike)*
  - » *Han Solo (same as POTF II 1997's Han Solo in Endor Gear with Blaster Pistol)*
  - » *Logray (same as POTF II 1998's Wicket & Logray with Staff, Medicine Pouch, and Spear)*
  - » *Rebel Trooper (same as Saga 2002's #33—Endor Rebel Soldier)*
  - » *Speeder Bike*
  - » *Wicket (same as POTF II 1998's Wicket & Logray with Staff, Medicine Pouch, and Spear)*
- » **NABOO FINAL CONFLICT (TOYS"R"US EXCLUSIVE)**
  - » *Battle Droid (same as POTJ 2000's Battle Droid [Boomer Damage])*
  - » *Captain Tarpals (modified from* Episode I *1999's Captain Tarpals with Electropole)*

- » *Gungan Soldier (same as POTJ 2000's Gungan Warrior)*
- » *Kaadu (with Battle Droid Blaster and Boomer)*
- » *Naboo Palace Guard (same as* Episode I *1999's Naboo Royal Guard)*

» SCREEN SCENES
- Jedi Council I
  - » *Ki-Adi-Mundi*
  - » *Qui-Gon Jinn*
  - » *Yoda*
- Jedi Council II
  - » *Eeth Koth*
  - » *Obi-Wan*
  - » *Plo Koon*
- Jedi Council III
  - » *Adi Gallia*
  - » *Anakin Skywalker*
  - » *Saesee Tiin*
- Jedi Council IV
  - » *Agen Kolar*
  - » *Shaak Ti*
  - » *Stass Allie*
- Mos Eisley Cantina I (Kmart exclusive)
  - » *Dr. Evazan*
  - » *Kitik Keed'kak*
  - » *Wuher*
- Mos Eisley Cantina II (Kmart exclusive)
  - » *Obi-Wan Kenobi*
  - » *Ponda Baba*
  - » *Zutton*

Vehicles

- Darth Vader's TIE Fighter (with Darth Vader)
- *Millennium Falcon* (Electronic Lights and Sounds)
- *Millennium Falcon* & *Millennium Falcon* Crew (Sam's Club exclusive with multi-pack of Chewbacca, Han Solo, Luke Skywalker, Obi-Wan

- Kenobi, C-3PO and R2-D2).
- TIE Fighter
- TIE Fighter & X-wing Fighter (Costco exclusive 2-Pack)
- Sandcrawler (with RA-7 Droid and two Jawas; Diamond exclusive)
- *Slave I* (with Boba Fett)
- X-wing Fighter
- Y-wing Fighter (with unique Rebel Alliance Pilot) (Toys"R"Us exclusive)

OTC "Vintage" packaging (aka. VOTC) (2004)

According to the action figures' package backs, these OTC vintage figures are "The finest recreations of the iconic *Star Wars* heroes and villains are back with incredible detail and premium features to commemorate each epic tale in the *Original Trilogy: A New Hope*, *The Empire Strikes Back*, and *Return of the Jedi*. And, as a tribute to the dedication of *Star Wars* fans everywhere, we are re-releasing elements of the original packaging that harken back to the creation of *Star Wars* action figures, which began over 25 years ago with the Original Trilogy. May the Force be with you!"

Regardless of why they were made, these superbly detailed action figures placed within iconic, vintage-style packaging would become a rousing success at retail, and so a recurring theme was born. A conceit that Hasbro would revisit intermittently until the release (and triumph) of Hasbro's "The Vintage Collection" (2010-2013).

» THE EMPIRE STRIKES BACK
- C-3PO
- Darth Vader
- Lando Calrissian
- Yoda

Luke Skywalker, 2004, [Vintage] Original Trilogy Collection [*A New Hope*], **$14-$22 MOC**. Beginning in 2004, Hasbro decided to tap into a retro chic motif and produce a gloriously designed series of three action figure assortments that would be highly detailed, ornately sculpted, and packaged within vintage, Kenner-style card backs. These toys were a smash hit, and the Vintage Original Trilogy Collection's success would lead to this style being appropriated again in 2006 with six more figures added to the Saga Collection's Vintage figure offerings (aka. "Vintage Saga Collection" [TVSC]). These two successful series proved the value of soliciting vintage-style figures, which led to The Vintage Collection (2010-2013). This series is considered the beginning of that sub-line, and collectors routinely purchase these figures to add to The Vintage Collection displays. Note that the VOTC figures came with outer packaging that protected the inner carded figure. They are a few dollars more valuable in this sealed packaging (not shown).

» **RETURN OF THE JEDI**
- Boba Fett
- Chewbacca
- R2-D2
- Stormtrooper

» **STAR WARS**
- Han Solo
- Luke Skywalker
- Obi-Wan Kenobi
- Princess Leia

» **12" ACTION FIGURES (VINTAGE-STYLE PACKAGING)**
- Boba Fett
- Chewbacca (K·B Toys exclusive)
- Luke Skywalker
- Stormtrooper

CHAPTER 11

Revenge of the Sith

Although the figures produced by Hasbro in this subline (2005-early 2006) were created a mere three years after *Attack of the Clones* characters infiltrated the *Star Wars* Saga assortments of 2002-2003, the detail, articulation, and accessories of the toys Hasbro produced for *Episode III: Revenge of the Sith* seemed light-years ahead of their precursor sister line. The spectacular designs of brand new yet immediately-iconic villains such as General Grievous, Count Dooku, and the other perpetrators of the infamous "Order 66" sold briskly at retail.

Unlike *Attack of the Clones*, the toys based upon this best-received film of the prequel trilogy (Rotten Tomatoes gives it a powerful 80 percent approval rating) still hold some decent value on the secondary market — although the demand is spotty and is not comparable to the desirability of vintage product (1977-1985) or the more modern, highly-articulated, well-designed releases of *The Clone Wars* (2008-2013) or The Vintage Collection (2010-2013) — two sub-lines too modern (and with values which fluctuate too fiercely) to be included within the text of this book.

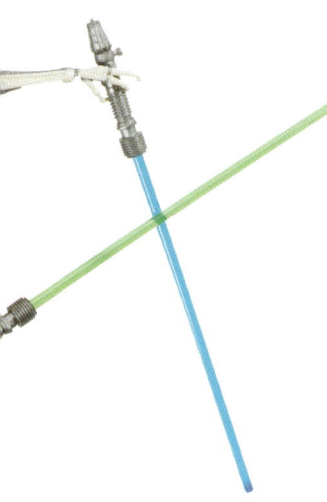

General Grievous, 12", 2005, *Revenge of the Sith*, **$70-$75 MISB**; **$25-$30 MLC**. One of Hasbro's monumental achievements in the 1:6 scale (12" action figures are rendered in 1/6 scale; 3-3/4" action figures are rendered in 1/18 scale), this *Revenge of the Sith* General Grievous figure is impressive in every possible way: from his articulated, segmented arms, which can hold a set of the four included lightsabers (which Grievous has scrounged from fallen Jedi Knights), to a thickly detailed soft goods cape: a truly impressive garment.

» ACTION FIGURES
- #01 Obi-Wan Kenobi (Slashing Attack!)
- #02 Anakin Skywalker (Lightsaber Attack!)
- #03 Yoda (Firing Cannon!)
- #04 Super Battle Droid (Firing Arm Blaster!)
- #05 Chewbacca (Wookie Rage!)
- #06 Clone Trooper (Quick Draw Action!)
  » *[standard colors]*
  » *[Shock Trooper colors]*
- #07 R2-D2 (Droid Attack!)
- #08 General Grevious' Bodyguard (Battle Attack!)
- #09 General Grevious (Four Lightsaber Attack!)
- #10 Mace Windu (Force Combat!)
- #11 Darth Vader (Lightsaber Attack!)
- #12 Emperor Palpatine (Firing Force Lightning!)
- #13 Count Dooku (Sith Lord)
- #14 Chancellor Palpatine (Supreme Chancellor)
- #15 Bail Organa (Republic Senator)
- #16 Plo Koon (Jedi Master)
- #17 Battle Droid (Separatist Army)
- #18 C-3PO (Protocol Droid)
- #19 Padmé (Republic Senator)
- #20 Agen Kolar (Jedi Master)
- #21 Shaak Ti (Jedi Master)
- #22 Kit Fisto (Jedi Master)
- #23 Royal Guard (Senate Security)
  » *Blue: Senate Guard, Coruscant*
  » *Red: Emperor's Royal Guard*
- #24 Mon Mothma (Republic Senator)
- #25 Tarfful (Firing Bowcaster!)
- #26 Yoda (Spinning Attack!)
- #27 Obi-Wan Kenobi (Jedi Kick!)
- #28 Anakin Skywalker (Slashing Attack!)
- #29 Ki-Adi-Mundi (Jedi Master)
- #30 Saesee Tiin (Jedi Master)

Royal Guard (Senate Security), blue Senate Guard, Coruscant, 2005, #23, *Revenge of the Sith*, **$6-$10 MOC**; Royal Guard (Senate Security), red Emperor's Royal Guard, 2005, #23, *Revenge of the Sith*, **$7-$12 MOC**; **$10 [each] MLC**. Hasbro's *Revenge of the Sith* line was remarkable for many reasons—one of the most important? The company finally began to recognize the power of offering "troop-builders" to the consumer. Realizing that diehard *Star Wars* fans were desperate to amass a variety of different troops to grow their Imperial army or navy, instead of simply offering a standard, stock Senate Guard for *ROTS* #23, Hasbro solicited two different elite soldiers: a blue Senate Guard for Coruscant, and a red Emperor's Royal Guard.

Clone Pilot (Firing Cannon!), black-and-silver variant, 2005, #34, *Revenge of the Sith*, **$9-$14 MOC** (top left); Clone Pilot (Firing Cannon!), white-and-gray variant, 2005, #34, *Revenge of the Sith*, **$6-$8 MOC** (top right).

- #31 Luminara Unduli (Jedi Master)
- #32 Aayla Secura (Jedi Knight)
- #33 Clone Commander (Battle Gear!)
- #34 Clone Pilot (Firing Cannon!)
- #35 Palpatine (Lightsaber Attack!)
- #36 General Grievous (Exploding Body!)
- #37 Vader's Medical Droid (Chopper Droid [DD-13])
- #38 AT-TE Tank Gunner (Clone Army)
- #39 Polis Massan (Medic)
- #40 Mas Amedda (Republic Senator)
- #41 Clone Trooper (Super-Articulated!)
- #42 Neimoidian Warrior (Neimoidian Blaster Attack!)
- #43 Wookie Warrior (Wookiee Battle Bash!)
  » *Light brown fur*
  » *Dark tan fur*
- #44 Destroyer Droid (Firing Arm-Blaster!)

The Clone Pilot possessed two variants: a common white-and-gray standard release that was featured in *Revenge of the Sith*, and an uncommon black-and-silver variant that was never featured in any film. Since obtaining the standard Clone Trooper figure is fairly inexpensive, many collectors choose to "troop build" these as pilots for their ships which were released ca. *ROTS*.

- #45 Tarkin (Governor)
- #46 Ask Aak ([Republic] Senator)
- #47 Meena Tillis ([Republic] Senator)
- #48 R2-D2 (Electronic Lights and Sounds!)
- #49 Commander Bacarra (Quick-Draw Attack!)
- #50 Anakin Skywalker (Battle Damage!)
- #51 Captain Antilles (Senate Security)
- #52 Jett Jukassa (Jedi Padawan)
- #53 Utapauan Warrior (Utapaun Security!)
- #54 AT-RT Driver (Missile-Firing Blaster!)
- #55 Obi-Wan Kenobi (With Pilot Gear!)
- #56 Mustafar Sentry (Spinning Energy Bolt!)
- #57 Commander Bly (Battle Gear!)
- #58 Wookiee Commando (Kashyyyk Battle Bash!)
- #59 Commander Gree (Battle Gear!)
- #60 Grievous' Bodyguard (Battle Attack!)
- #61 Passel Argente (Separatist Leader)

- #62 Cat Miin (Separatist) [Shu Mai's Aide]
- #63 Neimoidian Commander (Separatist Bodyguard)
- #64 R4-P17 (Rolling Action!) [Astromech Droid]
- #65 Tactical Ops Trooper (Vader's Legion!) [blue markings]
- #66 Plo Koon (Jedi Hologram Transmission)
- #67 Aayla Secura (Jedi Hologram Transmission)
- #68 Wookiee Heavy Gunner (Blast Attack!)

» BATTLE ARENA TWO-PACKS

- Bodyguard vs. Obi-Wan (Utapau Landing Platform)
- Dooku vs. Anakin (Trade Federation Cruiser)
- Sidious vs. Mace (Chancellor's Office)

» BATTLE PACKS

- Assault on Hoth
  - *General Veers*
  - *Probot*
  - *Snowtrooper (x3)*
- Clone Attack on Coruscant
  - *Clone Commander*
  - *Clone Trooper (x4)*
- Imperial Throne Room
  - *Emperor Royal Guard (x2)*
  - *Imperial Dignitary*
  - *Stormtrooper*
- Jedi Temple Assault
  - *Anakin Skywalker*
  - *Clone Pilot (x3)*
  - *Special Ops Troopers*
- Jedi vs. Sith
  - *Anakin Skywalker*
  - *Asajj Ventress*
  - *General Grievous*
  - *Obi-Wan Kenobi*
  - *Yoda*

- Jedi vs. Separatists
  - *Anakin Skywalker*
  - *Darth Maul*
  - *Jango Fett*
  - *Mace Windu*
  - *Obi-Wan Kenobi*
- Rebel vs. Empire
  - *Chewie*
  - *Darth Vader*
  - *Han Solo*
  - *Luke Skywalker*
  - *Stormtrooper*

» CREATURES
- Boga (with Obi-Wan Kenobi)

» DELUXE FIGURES
- Anakin Skywalker (Changes to Darth Vader)
- Chancellor Palpatine/Darth Sidious (Transformation)
- Clone Trooper (Firing Jet Backpack)
- Clone Troopers (3-pack, assorted colors)
- Crab Droid (with Moving Legs and Missile Launcher)
- Darth Vader (Rebuild Darth Vader)
- General Grievous (with Secret Lightsaber Attack)
- Obi-Wan Kenobi (with Force Jump Attack)
- Spider Droid (with Firing "Laser" Action)
- Stass Allie with BARC Speeder (with "Exploding" Action)
- Vulture Droid
- Yoda

ROTS "Evolutions" packaging (2005)

Utilizing a novel approach to solicit their action figure offerings, Hasbro decided to track the progress — encapsulate the evolution — of a *Star Wars* character over a period of time. Focusing on the most popular heroes and villains of the six existing movies, with the release of *Revenge of the Sith* the company finally had the opportunity to pillage every scene of both trilogies (and the Expanded Universe as well) to construct these remarkable three-figure progressions that allowed fans to witness a character's path of development in one single compact package.

- Anakin Skywalker to Darth Vader
  - » *Anakin Skywalker—Jedi Hero (*Episode II*)*
  - » *Anakin Skywalker—Clone Wars Commander (*Episode III*)*
  - » *Darth Vader—Evil Sith Lord (*Episode IV*)*
- Clone Trooper to Stormtrooper [Set #1—colorful paint applications]
  - » *Clone Trooper—The Clone Wars (*Episode II*)*
  - » *Clone Trooper—The Fall of the Republic (*Episode III*)*
  - » *Stormtrooper [Sandtooper]—The Rebellion (*Episode IV*)*
- Clone Trooper to Stormtrooper [Set #2—gray-toned paint applications]
  - » *Clone Trooper—The Clone Wars (*Episode II*)*
  - » *Clone Trooper—The Fall of the Republic (*Episode III*)*
  - » *Stormtrooper [Sandtooper]—The Rebellion (*Episode IV*)*
- The Sith
  - » *Darth Maul—The Sith Return (*Episode I*)*
  - » *Count Dooku—The Clone Wars (*Episode II*)*
  - » *Emperor Palpatine—The Republic Falls (*Episode III*)*

Clone Trooper (Super-Articulated!) [pictured bottom], 2005, #41, **$5-$8 MLC** (top); Clone Commander (Battle Gear!) [top], 2005, #23, **$6-$10 MOC** (middle); Commander Bacara (Quick-Draw Attack!) [opposite page], 2005, #23, **$5-$10 MOC**. The backbone of any good *Star Wars* fan's army whose collection began during the premiere of *Episode II* (2002), *Episode III* (2005), or *The Clone Wars* (2003, 2008) is often times a whopping big group of Clone Troopers. The difficulty usually comes from not being able to tell them apart. With the premiere of the super-articulated Clone Trooper in 2005 and the introduction of high level officers who've risen to the role of Commander, it would benefit *Star Wars* fans tremendously to educate themselves about armor (Phase I & II), armament, and rank—since some clones are more valuable than others.

Exclusives

- » (K·B TOYS)
  - Collector's Multi-Pack (nine figures + Silver Darth Vader)
- » (TARGET)
  - Clone Trooper (new markings)
  - Darth Vader (Lava Reflection)
  - Darth Vader (Duel at Mustafar)
  - Obi-Wan Kenobi (Duel at Mustafar)
  - Utapau Shadow Trooper
- » (TOYS"R"US)
  - Holographic Yoda (Kashyyyk Transmission)
  - Holographic Emperor Palpatine
- » (STAR WARS SHOP.COM)
  - Covert Ops Clone Trooper
- » (WALMART)
  - Commemorative *Episode III* DVD Collection* 1 of 3 (Jedi Knights)
    - » *Anakin Skywalker*
    - » *Mace Windu*
    - » *Obi-Wan Kenobi*
  - Commemorative *Episode III* DVD Collection* 2 of 3 (Sith Lords)
    - » *Count Dooku*
    - » *Darth Vader*
    - » *Emperor Palpatine*
  - Commemorative *Episode III* DVD Collection* 3 of 3 (Clone Troopers)
    - » *Clone Trooper x3 (unique paint scheme)*

  Note: These three multi-packs do not include a Star Wars DVD.

- » PLAYSETS
  - Mustafar Final Duel (includes Obi-Wan Kenobi and Darth Vader)

- Mustafar Final Duel (includes 4 Bonus Figures; Sam's Club exclusive)

» SNEAK PREVIEW FIGURES
- (1 of 4): General Grievous
- (2 of 4): Tion Medon
- (3 of 4): Wookiee Warrior
- (4 of 4): R4-G9

» SNEAK PREVIEW VEHICLES
- Anakin's Jedi Starfighter

» VEHICLES
- Anakin's Jedi Starfighter (with Anakin Skywalker; Toys"R"Us exclusive)
- ARC-170 Starfighter
- AT-RT (with AT-RT Driver)
- Barc Speeder (with Barc Trooper)
- Droid Tri-Fighter
- Obi-Wan's Jedi Starfighter
- Obi-Wan's Jedi Starfighter (with Obi-Wan Kenobi; Toys"R"Us exclusive)
- Grievous' Wheel Bike (with General Grievous)
- Plo Koon's Jedi Starfighter
- Republic Gunship
- Wookiee Flyer (with Wookiee Warrior)

» 12" ACTION FIGURES
- Anakin Skywalker/Darth Vader (Ultimate Villain)
- Barriss Offee
- Chewbacca (K·B Toys exclusive)
- Clone Trooper
- Darth Sidious
- General Grievous
- Shaak Ti

CHAPTER 12

The Saga Collection

For the very first time in Hasbro's history, the company created a sub-line of *Star Wars* product that consolidated characters, accessories, creatures, playsets, vehicles, and weapon systems under one banner: "*Star Wars*: The Saga Collection," produced from 2006-2007. This collector-dedicated toy line, with its spectacular silver-and-black packaging design, captured the hearts and minds of dedicated aficionados and casual fans alike. Released in theme-based assortments based on familiar settings within the two film trilogies (Bespin, Hoth, Naboo, etc.), the *Star Wars*: Saga Collection product still retains some value on the secondary market.

Furthermore, each action figure in the line was released with an added bonus: an "exclusive hologram figure!" that provided collectors with an added incentive to "collect 'em all"! Standing at under 2 inches tall, these semi-translucent blue or red hologram figures are necessary purchases for every diehard completionist: those collectors who are compelled to obtain one of every *Star Wars* toy. The mini-figures available in both blue and red are Han Solo, Luke Skywalker, Obi-Wan Kenobi, Queen Amidala, Rebel Trooper, Yoda, Boba Fett, Count Dooku, Darth Maul, Darth Vader, Emperor Palpatine, and a Stormtrooper. That means—besides those pewter-looking "chase" hologram figures, there are 24 total figures available to collect.

Mace Windu's Jedi Starfighter, 2006, Saga Collection [*The Clone Wars*], **$9-$13 MLC**; Mace Windu (The Episode III Heroes and Villains Collection), 2006, (10 of 12), Saga Collection *[Revenge of the Sith]*, **$3-$5 MLC**; R4-M6 (Mace Windu's Astromech Droid), 2006, #74, Saga Collection [Expanded Universe] (Walmart exclusive), **$8-$14 MLC**. When purchasing a Jedi Starfighter, many collectors are compelled to track down the vehicle-appropriate pilot, and then obtain the pilot's relevant astromech droid. Here, the entire set of all three toys came from The Saga Collection (TSC): Mace Windu, his purple-highlighted Jedi Starfighter, and R4-M6 (his attending droid) could all be obtained MLC for between **$20 and $32**. Packaged, it would be roughly between **$50 and $65** in total. Oddly enough, many collectors would actually pay more money for all three of these items together than if they were bought separately: for *Star Wars* fans, it's not the getting … it's the having.

Action Figures

(SERIES ONE—BATTLE OF CARKOON)
- SAGA-001: Princess Leia (Boushh Disguise)
- SAGA-002: Han Solo (Carbonite)
- SAGA-003: Bib Fortuna
- SAGA-004: Barada (Skiff Guard)
- SAGA-005: Chewbacca (Boushh Prisoner)
- SAGA-006: Boba Fett

(SERIES TWO—BATTLE OF HOTH)
- SAGA-007: General Veers
- SAGA-008: Major Bren Derlin
- SAGA-009: AT-AT Driver
- SAGA-010: R2-D2
- SAGA-011: Snowtrooper
- SAGA-012: General Rieekan
- SAGA-013: Darth Vader
- SAGA-014: Power Droid

(SERIES THREE—BATTLE OF GEONOSIS)
- SAGA-015: Sora Bulq
- SAGA-016: Sun Fac
- SAGA-017: C-3PO (with Battle Droid head)
- SAGA-018: Poggle the Lesser
- SAGA-019: Yoda
- SAGA-020: Jango Fett
- SAGA-021: Scorch (Republic Commando)

(SERIES FOUR—BATTLE OF CORUSCANT)
- SAGA-022: Firespeeder Pilot
- SAGA-023: Lushros Dofine
- SAGA-024: Clone Commander Cody
- SAGA-025: Anakin Skywalker
- SAGA-026: Clone Trooper (Utapau)
- SAGA-027: Holographic Ki-Adi-Mundi
- SAGA-028: Obi-Wan Kenobi
- SAGA-029: Foul Moudama
- SAGA-030: General Grievous

(SERIES FIVE—ESCAPE FROM MOS EISLEY)
- SAGA-031: Momaw Nadon

Princess Leia (Boushh Disguise) (Battle of Carkoon), 2006, #001, Saga Collection, [*Return of the Jedi*], **$8-$11 MOC**. Part of an ingenious assortment that would unite all six films under one sub-line, *Star Wars*: The Saga Collection was collector-friendly and focused on the most famous battles that took place within the two trilogies. With its retro silver-and-black package design, many of these accessories, creatures, and action figures—such as this new interpretation of Princess Leia—still hold their value and a few select items command a bit more than their original retail prices.

Han Solo (Carbonite) (Battle of Carkoon), 2006, #002, Saga Collection, [*Return of the Jedi*], **$7-$10 MOC**. Although action figures from The Saga Collection do not exhibit the same amount of detail or articulation as those *Star Wars* characters produced after 2008, they still capture the most iconic elements and details of certain characters—such as this version of Han Solo with his requisite block of carbonite.

General Veers (Battle of Hoth), 2006, #002, Saga Collection, [*The Empire Strikes Back*], **$12-$15 MOC; $7-$10 MLC**. One of the most memorable of all Imperial officers, the shrewd and cunning visage of General Veers is expertly captured in this Saga Collection release. With a removable helmet, chest armor, and requisite E-11 Imperial blaster, this figure still remains desirable on the secondary market.

AT-AT Driver (Battle of Hoth), 2006, #009, Saga Collection, [*The Empire Strikes Back*], **$10-$12 MOC; $7-$10 MLC**. Taking yet another major leap forward in terms of detail and articulation, The Saga Collection's swivel elbows, swivel hands, articulated hips, ball-joined shoulders, and ball-joined neck—such as those exhibited with this AT-AT Driver figure—allows collectors to continue pillaging TSC trooper action figures on the secondary market.

Firespeeder Pilot (Battle of Coruscant), 2006, #009, Saga Collection, [*Revenge of the Sith*], **$6-$8 MOC**. Sometimes Hasbro decided to capture all-new figures in TSC, and therefore they birthed the infinitely cool looking Firespeeder Pilot—a trooper whose job it is to address the conflagration after two famous Jedi knights crash land General Grievous' flagship, *The Invisible Hand*, onto the planet Coruscant.

Foul Moudama (Battle of Coruscant), 2006, #029, Saga Collection, [Expanded Universe] (*Clone Wars* [animated]), **$6-$10 MOC**. One of the few action figures from the early iteration of the stylized, animated *Clone Wars* cartoon that was not solicited in 2003's *Clone Wars* toy line.

- SAGA-032: R5-D4
- SAGA-033: Hem Dazon
- SAGA-034: Garindan
- SAGA-035: Han Solo
- SAGA-036: Luke Skywalker
- SAGA-037: Sandtrooper

(SERIES SIX—BESPIN CONFESSION)
- SAGA-038: Darth Vader

(SERIES SEVEN—BATTLE OF ENDOR)
- SAGA-039: Chief Chirpa
- SAGA-040: Moff Jerjerrod
- SAGA-041: Death Star Gunner
- SAGA-042: C-3PO
- SAGA-043: Emperor Palpatine
- SAGA-044: Luke Skywalker
- SAGA-045: Darth Vader
- SAGA-046: Rebel Trooper I (
  - » *'Caucasian')*
  - » *('African-American')*
- SAGA-047: Obi-Wan Kenobi

(SERIES EIGHT—*THE PHANTOM MENACE* [ASSORTED BATTLES])
- SAGA-048: Holographic Darth Maul
- SAGA-049: Rep Been
- SAGA-050: Naboo Soldier
- SAGA-051: Dud Bolt & Mars Guo
- SAGA-052: Gragra

(SERIES ONE—REPACKS & REPAINTS)
- SAGA-053: Sith Training Darth Maul
- SAGA-054: Chewbacca with Electronic C-3PO
- SAGA-055: Kit Fisto
- SAGA-056: Holographic Clone Commander Cody
- SAGA-057: Clone Trooper (442nd Siege Battalion)
- SAGA-058: R5-J2
- SAGA-059: Clone Trooper (Fifth Fleet Security)

- SAGA-060: Clone Trooper Sergeant
- SAGA-061: Super Battle Droid
- SAGA-062: Battle Droids

(SERIES TWO—REPACKS & REPAINTS)

- SAGA-063: Holographic Obi-Wan Kenobi
- SAGA-064: Commander Appo
- SAGA-065: Elite Corps Clone Trooper
- SAGA-066: R4-K5 (Darth Vader's Astromech Droid)
- SAGA-067: Padmé Amidala
- SAGA-068: Combat Engineer Clone Trooper
- SAGA-069: Yarael Poof

(SERIES THREE—REPACKS & REPAINTS [WALMART EXCLUSIVES])

- SAGA-070: Aurra Sing
- SAGA-071: Kitik Keed'kak
- SAGA-072: Nabrun Leids & Kabe
- SAGA-073: Labria
- SAGA-074: R4-M6 (Mace Windu's Astromech Droid)

Action Figures

» ULTIMATE GALACTIC HUNT (CHASE FIGURE VARIANTS)

Note: Each of the following ten (10) variant action figures bear exactly the same design as their more commonly-released counterparts. However, the packaging for the figures is embossed with silver, while the included posing stand/base is rendered in silver plastic with black lettering. Furthermore, the exclusive hologram figure that is included within each package is also molded in silver and washed with black paint: giving it a valuable-looking veneer (as opposed to the standard 24 red or blue characters).

- AT-AT Driver
- Anakin Skywalker
- Boba Fett
- Clone Commander Cody
- Darth Vader
- General Grievous
- Han Solo (Carbonite)

Moff Jerjerrod (Battle of Endor), 2006, #040, Saga Collection, [*Return of the Jedi*], **$10-$13 MOC**. Tasked by Darth Vader to "redouble his efforts" when constructing the second Death Star in anticipation of a visit by Emperor Palpatine, Admiral Moff Jerjerrod was both competent and capable-but ultimately doomed when the Rebels successfully detonated the Death Star II's reactor core.

Combat Engineer Clone Trooper, 2006, #068, Saga Collection, [Expanded Universe (during *Revenge of the Sith*], **$8-$10 MOC; $4-$6 MLC**. The Combat Engineer Clone Trooper is assigned to anywhere armored ground troopers are required. As a member of the 38th Armored Division, Combat Engineer Battalion, they also work on fortified war machines.

Yarael Poof, 2006, #069, Saga Collection, [Expanded Universe (during *The Phantom Menace*)], **$10-$14 MOC**. One of the oddest-looking Jedi and master of the Jedi High Council, thanks to his peculiar race (is a Quermian), Jedi Master Yarael Poof reportedly possessed the slight telepathic abilities granted to all of the members of this species. Poof has presented lectures to instruct padawans on how to bend enemies to their will; he was yet another in a long line of Jedi who had a brief appearance in a film yet were translated into plastic form.

- Obi-Wan Kenobi
- Scorch (Republic Commando)
- Snowtrooper

Battle Packs

- Battle Above the Sarlaac
    - *Boba Fett*
    - *Han Solo*
    - *Lando Calrissian*
    - *Luke Skywalker*
    - *Weequay Skiff Guard*
- Jedi vs. Darth Sidious
    - *Agen Kolar*
    - *Darth Sidious*
    - *Kit Fisto*
    - *Mace Windu*
    - *Saesee Tiin*
- Sith Lord Attack
    - *Battle Droid*
    - *Battle Droid Security*
    - *Darth Maul*
    - *Obi-Wan Kenobi*
    - *Qui-Gon Jinn*

- » (TARGET EXCLUSIVES)
  - Mace Windu's Attack Battalion
    - » *Clone Commander*
    - » *Clone Troopers (x3)*
    - » *Mace Windu*
  - Skirmish in the Senate
    - » *Emperor Palpatine*
    - » *Senate Pod*
    - » *Shocktroopers (x2)*
    - » *Yoda*
- » (TOYS"R"US EXCLUSIVE)
  - The Hunt For Grievous
    - » *Captain Gordo*
    - » *Clone Troopers (x3)*
    - » *Heavy Gunner Clone Trooper*

Exclusive Figures

- » (WALMART)
  - Early Bird Certificate Package (Certificate, Display Stand, Membership Card, Stickers, "Hyperspace" Trial Membership Card, Pre-Addressed Envelope)
  - Early Bird Kit (with Chewbacca, Luke Skywalker, Princess Leia, and R2-D2)
  - Separation of the Twins: Leia Organa (with Bail Organa)
  - Separation of the Twins: Luke Skywalker (with Obi-Wan Kenobi)
- » (TARGET)
  - General Grievous (Demise of Grievous)
- » (ULTIMATE GALACTIC HUNT MAIL-AWAY)
  - George Lucas: (In Stormtrooper Disguise)
- » (CONVENTION EXCLUSIVES)
  - 501st Stormtrooper (San Diego Comic Con)
- » (INTERNET EXCLUSIVES)
  - Shadow Stormtrooper (StarWarsShop.com)

Multi-Packs

- » (ENTERTAINMENT EARTH EXCLUSIVES)
  - Astromech Droid Pack Series I
    - » *R4-A22*
    - » *R2-C4*
    - » *R2-Q2*
    - » *R3-T2*
    - » *R3-T6*
  - Astromech Droid Pack Series II
    - » *R2-A6*
    - » *R2-M5*
    - » *R2-X2*
    - » *R3-Y2*
    - » *R4-E1*
- » (PREVIEWS EXCLUSIVES)
  - The Hunt for *The Millennium Falcon*: Bounty Hunter Pack
    - » *4-LOM*
    - » *Boba Fett*
    - » *Bossk*
    - » *Darth Vader*
    - » *Dengar*
    - » *IG-88*
    - » *Zuckuss*
- » (STARWARSSHOP.COM EXCLUSIVES)
  - Lucas Collector Set
    - » *Baron Papanoida*
    - » *Chi Eekway*
    - » *Terr Taneel*
    - » *Zett Jukassa*
- » (WALMART EXCLUSIVES)
  - Commemorative Episode IV DVD Collection*
  Star Wars: A New Hope
    - » *Darth Vader*
    - » *Luke Skywalker*
    - » *Obi-Wan Kenobi*

- Commemorative Episode V DVD Collection*
  Star Wars: The Empire Strikes Back
  - » *Chewbacca*
  - » *Han Solo*
  - » *Stormtrooper*
- Commemorative Episode VI DVD Collection*
  Star Wars: Return of the Jedi
  - » *C-3PO*
  - » *Emperor Palpatine*
  - » *Luke Skywalker*
  - » *R2-D2*

Note: These three multi-packs do not include a Star Wars DVD.

- Value Packs (combining two action figures within a new clamshell case)
  - » *Multiple combinations*

Scene Packs

- Death Star Briefing
  - » *Admiral Motti*
  - » *Chief Bast*
  - » *Colonel Wulf Yularen*
  - » *General Tagge*
  - » *Grand Moff Tarkin*
  - » *Officer Cass*
- Republic Commando Delta Squad (Expanded Universe)
  - » *Delta Three-Eight*
  - » *Fixer*
  - » *Geonosian Warriors (x2)*
  - » *Scorch*
  - » *Sev*
  - » *Sun Fac*

Vintage Saga Collection

- Biker Scout
- Greedo
- Han Solo (Trench Coat)
- Luke Skywalker (X-Wing Pilot)
- Sand People

Death Star Briefing (Previews exclusive), 2006, Saga Collection [*A New Hope*], **$62-$70 MIB**. The Previews exclusive 'Scene Pack' known as the Death Star Briefing featured one of the more unforgettable scenes from *A New Hope*. The set is comprised of Darth Vader, Grand Moff Tarkin, and a small coterie of Imperial officers who were totally at the mercy of these two Imperial heavies: Admiral Motti, Chief Bast, Colonel Wulf Yularen, General Tagge, and Officer Cass.

The Episode III Greatest Battles Collection

- 1 of 14: 501st Legion Trooper
- 2 of 14: AT-TE Tank Gunner
- 3 of 14: C-3PO
- 4 of 14: Count Dooku
- 5 of 14: Royal Guard (Senate Security, blue variant)
- 6 of 14: Padmé
- 7 of 14: R4-G9
- 8 of 14: Kit Fisto
- 9 of 14: Wookiee Warrior
- 10 of 14: R2-D2 (Electronic)
- 11 of 14: Shocktrooper
- 12 of 14: Obi-Wan Kenobi
- 13 of 14: Emperor Palpatine
- 14 of 14: Clone Commander
  - » *(green color scheme)*
  - » *(red color scheme)*

Due to its nature as an exclusive release, with its magnificent packaging and never-before-released characters, it still commands respect on the secondary market, with loose sets selling for nearly as much as boxed samples: **$45-55 MLC**. Col. Wulf Yularen—the rarest figure in the set—may sell for as much as **$25 MLC**; he is in high demand.

The Episode III Heroes & Villains Collection

- 1 of 12: Darth Vader
- 2 of 12: Anakin Skywalker
- 3 of 12: Yoda
- 4 of 12: Commander Bacara
- 5 of 12: Clone Trooper
- 6 of 12: Clone Pilot (Shadow Pilot)
- 7 of 12: Chewbacca
- 8 of 12: Obi-Wan Kenobi
- 9 of 12: General Grievous
- 10 of 12: Mace Windu
- 11 of 12: R2-D2
- 12 of 12: Destroyer Droid

Vehicles/Accessories

- Anakin's Jedi Starfighter (re-solicited in Saga Collection package [as opposed to *ROTS*])
- Darth Vader's TIE Advanced Fighter

- Droid Tri-Fighter (re-solicited in Saga Collection package [as opposed to *ROTS*])
- General Grievous' Wheel Bike (re-solicited in Saga Collection package [as opposed to *ROTS*])
- Mace Windu's Jedi Starfighter
- Obi-Wan's Jedi Starfighter (re-solicited in Saga Collection package [as opposed to *ROTS*])

» (TARGET EXCLUSIVES)
- TIE Fighter (2005) (with TIE Fighter Pilot) [with movie-accurate, larger wings]
- Imperial Shuttle (with Darth Vader and Royal Guard)
- Kit Fisto's Jedi Starfighter
- Rogue Two Snowspeeder (with Zev Senesca)

» (TOYS"R"US EXCLUSIVES)
- *Millennium Falcon* (2005)
- Endor AT-AT (with AT-AT Driver and Biker Scout)
- Luke Skywalker's X-Wing Fighter (with Luke Skywalker, removable moss, etc.)
- Republic Gunship (*Clone Wars* Deco)
- TIE Fighter (2006)

▶ Biker Scout, 2006, [Vintage] Saga Collection [*The Return of the Jedi*], **$8-$13 MOC**. With a mere six figures solicited in the Saga Collection's Vintage figure offerings (aka. "Vintage Saga Collection" [TVSC]), these iconic characters tested the water for Hasbro and proved something that comes as second nature during the past few years: collectors love retro styling. Packaged on Kenner card backs and using the defunct company's old school silver-and-black packaging, these toys flew off the shelves. And still hold some semblance of value nearly one decade later.

PICKER'S POCKET GUIDE: **STAR WARS TOYS** 177

CHAPTER 13

Anniversary Collection

Due to the overwhelming response of *Star Wars* aficionados to the Collector's Coins included within Kenner's vintage Power of the Force packages, Hasbro decided to solicit the same promotion in a modern toy line, from late 2006-2008: each newly released *Star Wars* 30th Anniversary action figure contained a silver, chrome-plated Collector Coin.

As delineated on the figures' package backs, the promotion's description reads as follows: "Now seasoned collectors and recent arrivals to the galaxy can experience the excitement of a new series of *Star Wars* collector coins. Depicting characters and scenes from the entire six-film epic as well as the Expanded Universe, these coins have been re-created in the original size - but with some fresh new twists. This special album has slots to display all 60 3-3/4-inch figure coins. You will also find extra spaces for duplicates or promotional coins that may be produced over the course of the year. Enjoy the hunt for these truly special coins!"

Darth Vader's Sith Starfighter, 2006, 30th Anniversary Collection [Expanded Universe: The Rise of Darth Vader], **$16-$20 MLC;** Darth Vader (Bespin Confession), 2006, #38, *Star Wars* Saga [*The Empire Strikes Back*], **$8-$10 MLC;** R4-K5 (Darth Vader's Astromech Droid), 2006, #66, *Star Wars* Saga [Expanded Universe], **$10-$14 MLC**. One of the great challenges of collecting *Star Wars* action figures is not only netting your favorite figures and villains for play and display, but capturing the precise figures and vehicles needed to set a particular "scene"— whether the scene is remembered from one of the six canonical films (*Episodes I-VI*) or from the Expanded Universe (EU). When purchasing one of the franchise's signature vehicles, in this case, the Jedi Starfighter (aka the Sith Starfighter—from TAC), the collector could then track down the vehicle-appropriate pilot (TSC), and then match the pilot with the character's favored astromech attendant (TSC). Here, the craft was modified for Darth Vader's personal use, and as such expertly accommodated the Dark Lord of the Sith and his handpicked Astromech droid, R4-K5. Thanks to Hasbro engineering, the "droid socket" that appears on the middle of the starfighter's left wing allowed kids to pop in their astromech of choice (or utilize the "droid shell" included with the vehicle to simulate the appearance of a full droid). From Obi-Wan Kenobi to Aayla Secura, from Anakin Skywalker to Mace Windu, this vehicle was a masterpiece of Hasbro engineering, allowing fans to repeat this process many times over.

Action Figures

2007

(SERIES 1–*REVENGE OF THE SITH*)
- 30-01: Darth Vader & 30th Anniversary Coin Album (album allows fans to collect and display)
- 30-02: Galactic Marine
- 30-03: Mustafar Lava Miner
- 30-04: R2-D2
- 30-05: Obi-Wan Kenobi
- 30-06: Mace Windu
- 30-07: Airborne Trooper
- 30-08: Super Battle Droid
- 30-09: McQuarrie Signature Series: Concept Stormtrooper

(SERIES 2—BATTLE OF YAVIN)
- 30-10: Rebel Honor Guard (Yavin)
- 30-11: Han Solo (Smuggler)
- 30-12: Luke Skywalker (Yavin Ceremony)
- 30-13: Death Star Trooper
- 30-14: Biggs Darklighter (Rebel Pilot)
- 30-15: McQuarrie Signature Series: Concept Boba Fett

(SERIES THREE—*A NEW HOPE*)
- 30-16: Darth Vader (Sith Lord)
- 30-17: Biggs Darklighter (Tosche Station)
- 30-18: Luke Skywalker (Moisture Farmer)
- 30-19: Jawa & LIN Droid (Tatooine Scavenger)
- 30-20: Imperial Stormtrooper (Galactic Empire)
- 30-21: McQuarrie Signature Series: Concept Chewbacca
- 30-22: M'iiyoom Onith (Hementhe)
- 30-23: Elis Helrot (Givin)

(SERIES FOUR—*RETURN OF THE JEDI*)
- 30-24: Boba Fett (Animated Debut)
- 30-25: Luke Skywalker (Jedi Knight)
- 30-26: CZ-4 (CZ-Series Droid)

> ### Picker's Tip
>
> This sub-line of figures sold particularly well since pack-in promotions that harken back to the original vintage line of toys (1977-1985) always seem to spark interest among die-hard collectors.

- 30-27: Umpass-Stay (Klatooinian)
- 30-28: McQuarrie Signature Series: Concept Darth Vader
- 30-29: Hermi Odle (Baragwin)
- 30-30: C-3PO & Salacious Crumb (Jabba's Servants)

(SERIES FIVE—EXPANDED UNIVERSE)

- 30-31: Roron Corobb (Jedi Knight)
- 30-32: Yoda & Kybuck (Jedi Master)
- 30-33: Anakin Skywalker (Jedi Knight)
- 30-34: Darth Revan (Sith Lord)
- 30-35: Darth Malak (Sith Lord)
- 30-36: Pre-Cyborg Grievous (Kaleesh Warlord Qymaen jai Sheelal)
- 30-37: McQuarrie Signature Series: Concept Starkiller Hero

(SERIES SIX—*THE EMPIRE STRIKES BACK*)

- 30-38: Han Solo (with Torture Rack)
- 30-39: Lando Calrissian (Smuggler Outfit)
- 30-40: General McQuarrie (Rebel Officer)
- 30-41: 4-LOM (Bounty Hunter)
- 30-42: McQuarrie Signature Series: Concept Snowtrooper

(SERIES SEVEN—*RETURN OF THE JEDI*)

- 30-43: Romba & Graak (Ewok Warriors)
- 30-44: Tycho Celchu (A-Wing Pilot)
- 30-45: Anakin Skywalker (Jedi Spirit)
- 30-46: R2-D2 (with Cargo Net)
- 30-47: McQuarrie Signature Series: Concept Han Solo

McQuarrie Signature Series Concept Stormtrooper, 2007, #09, 30th Anniversary Collection, **$10-$14 MOC**, **$8-$10 MLC**; McQuarrie Signature Series Concept Snowtrooper, 2007, #42, 30th Anniversary Collection, **$8-$11 MOC**, **$6-$9 MLC**. Showcasing the pre-production proposals of one of the preeminent designers of his (or any) era, the Ralph McQuarrie (June 13, 1929 – March 3, 2012) Signature Series action figures—such as this Stormtrooper and Snowtrooper—who were featured in The 30th Anniversary Collection will always be in demand on the secondary market for around **$8-20 MOC**, and are described on the toys' card back as follows: "The vivid imagination of conceptual artist Ralph McQuarrie brought to life the characters and worlds envisioned by George Lucas. McQuarrie's paintings and drawings were instrumental in the push to bring Lucas's saga to the big screen, giving shape and form to a multitude of fantastic individuals, creatures, planets and technology encompassed in this epic tale." Hasbro deigned these action figures "…in collaboration with [Ralph] McQuarrie himself, this remarkable action figure series pays tribute to the man whose art defined some of the most memorable characters in film history."

(SERIES 7.5—REPAINTS)
- 30-48: Darth Vader (Hologram)
- 30-49: Clone Trooper (7th Legion Trooper)
- 30-50: Clone Trooper (Hawkbat Battalion)
- 30-51: R2-B1 (Astromech Droid)
- 30-52: Naboo Soldier (Royal Naboo Army)
- 30-53: Rebel Vanguard Trooper (Star Wars: Battlefront)
- 30-54: Pax Bonkik (Rodian Podracer Mechanic)

(SERIES EIGHT—*ATTACK OF THE CLONES*)
- 30-55: Clone Trooper (Training Fatigues)
- 30-56: Padmé Amidala (Naboo Senator)
- 30-57: Jango Fett (Bounty Hunter)
- 30-58: Voolvif Monn (Jedi Master)
- 30-59: Destroyer Droid (Droideka)
- 30-60: McQuarrie Signature Series: Concept Rebel Trooper

2008

(SERIES ONE—*REVENGE OF THE SITH*)
- 08-01: Obi-Wan Kenobi
- 08-02: Darth Vader
- 08-03: Commander Gree
- 08-04: Kashyyyk Trooper
- 08-05: Tri-Droid
- 08-06: 2-1B (Surgical Droid)
- 08-07: Po Nudo
- 08-08: Mustafar Panning Droid

(SERIES TWO—*THE FORCE UNLEASHED**)
- 08-09: Imperial EVO Trooper
- 08-10: Imperial Jumptrooper
- 08-11: Maris Brood
- 08-12: Darth Vader (Battle Damage)
- 08-13: Rahm Kota
- 08-14: Shadow Guard
- 08-15: Juno Eclipse

*The characters in this series featured prominently in Lucasfilm's *The Force Unleashed* video game.

Action Figures — Ultimate Galactic Hunt

Note: The following twelve action figures — characters from the standard seventy-five assorted characters — were part of the "Ultimate Galactic Hunt" promotion, where each was available on a card with gold-bordered "Star Wars" logo instead of the standard silver. These figures also came with a gold-colored Collector Coin in place of the regular silver currency.

- 30-02: Galactic Marine
- 30-04: R2-D2
- 30-06: Mace Windu
- 30-07: Airborne Trooper
- 30-09: McQuarrie Signature Series: Concept Stormtrooper
- 30-11: Han Solo (Smuggler)
- 30-12: Luke Skywalker (Yavin Ceremony)
- 30-14: Biggs Darklighter (Rebel Pilot)
- 30-15: McQuarrie Signature Series: Concept Boba Fett
- 30-16: Darth Vader (Sith Lord)
- 30-21: McQuarrie Signature Series: Concept Chewbacca
- 30-24: Boba Fett (Animated Debut)

» BATTLE PACKS
- Battle of Geonosis
  » *Aayla Secura*
  » *Count Dooku*
  » *Jango Fett*
  » *Obi-Wan Kenobi*
  » *Super Battle Droid*
- Battle on Mygeeto
  » *Clone Commander Bacara*
  » *Ki-Adi-Mundi*
  » *Galactic Marine*
  » *Super Battle Droid*
  » *Tri-Droid*
- Betrayal on Bespin

- *Boba Fett*
  - *Chewbacca*
  - *Darth Vader*
  - *Han Solo*
  - *Princess Leia*
- Capture of *Tantive IV*
  - *Darth Vader*
  - *Rebel Trooper (x2)*
  - *Stromtrooper (x2)*
- Clone Attack on Coruscant (same exact set as released in 2005 *ROTS*)
  - *Clone Commander*
  - *Clone Trooper (x4)*
- Droid Factory Capture
  - *Anakin Skywalker*
  - *C-3PO*
  - *Destroyer Droid*
  - *Jango Fett*
  - *R2-D2*
- Jedi Training on Dagobah
  - *Luke Skywalker*
  - *R2-D2*
  - *Spirit of Darth Vader*
  - *Spirit of Obi-Wan Kenobi*
  - *Yoda*
- Jedi vs. Darth Sidious
  - *Agen Kolar*
  - *Darth Sidious*
  - *Kit Fisto*
  - *Mace Windu*
  - *Saesee Tiin*
- Jedi vs. Sith
  - *Anakin Skywalker*
  - *Asajj Ventress*
  - *General Grievous*

- » *Obi-Wan Kenobi*
- » *Yoda*
- The Hunt for Grievous
  - » *Captain Fordo*
  - » *Clone Trooper (x3)*
  - » *Heavy Gunner Clone Trooper*

» [TARGET EXCLUSIVES]
- Ambush on Ilum
  - » *C-3PO*
  - » *Chameleon Droid #1*
  - » *Chameleon Droid #2 (with Cloaking Effect)*
  - » *Padmé Amidala*
  - » *R2-D2*
- ARC-170 Elite Squad
  - » *ARC-170 Trooper #1*
  - » *ARC-170 Trooper #2*
  - » *Astromech Droid [R4-C7]*
  - » *Clone Trooper Pilot #1*
  - » *Clone Trooper Pilot #2*
- AT-RT Assault Squad
  - » *AT-RT vehicle (x2)*
  - » *AT-RT Driver (x2)*
  - » *Clone Commander*
- Attack on Kashyyyk
  - » *Darth Vader*
  - » *Stormtrooper (x2)*
  - » *Wookiee Warriors (x2)*
- Battle Rancor (with Felucian Rider and Saddle)
  - » *Battle Rancor*
  - » *Felucian Warrior/Rider*
- Betrayal on Felucia
  - » *Aayla Secura*
  - » *Clone Troopers (x3)*
  - » *Commander Bly*
- Ultimate Battle Pack: The Battle of Endor
  - » *AT-ST vehicle*

- » *AT-ST Driver*
- » *Biker Scout #1*
- » *Biker Scout #2*
- » *Chewbacca*
- » *Han Solo*
- » *Large Log (x2)*
- » *Oochee*
- » *Speeder Bike vehicle (x2)*
- » *Stormtrooper*
- » *Widdle Warrick (Wicket's brother)*
- Ultimate Battle Pack: The Battle of Hoth
  - » *AT-ST vehicle*
  - » *AT-ST Driver*
  - » *Han Solo*
  - » *Laser Turret*
  - » *Luke Skywalker*
  - » *Rebel Officer (Major Bren Derlin)*
  - » *Rebel Trooper*
  - » *Snowtrooper (x3)*

» (TOYS"R"US EXCLUSIVES)
- Bantha with Tusken Raiders
  - » *Bantha*
  - » *Massiff*
  - » *Tusken Raider (Female with Child [Uli-ah])*
  - » *Tusken Raider (Rider)*
  - » *Tusken Raider (Sniper)*
- Hoth Patrol
  - » *Luke Skywalker*
  - » *Tauntaun*
  - » *Wampa*
- STAP Attack
  - » *Battle Droid Pilot (x2)*
  - » *Super Battle Droid*
  - » *STAP vehicle (x2; with Support Stand [x2])*

» (WALMART EXCLUSIVES)
- Treachery on Saleucami

- » *BARC Speeder Bike (x2)*
- » *Clone Trooper*
- » *Commander Neyo*

TAC, "Comic Packs" packaging (2006-2008)

When releasing these, the first series of Star Wars: Comic Packs (a comic book reprint packaged with two action figures who were prominently featured in the book's narrative), Hasbro mined their hundred+ issues of Marvel Comics' original original Expanded Universe (EU) interpretation of the *Star Wars* canon (July 1977-September 1986, issue #'s 1-107), as well as the many different *Star Wars* titled produced by Dark Horse Comics in the 1990's and the 2000s, with *Crimson Empire, Empire, Infinities, Purge, Republic, Revenge of the Sith,* and *Star Wars: Tales*. Many of these two-packs are highly prized on the secondary market and command an exorbitant amount of money.

Comic Packs

2006

- 01: Carnor Jax & Kir Kanos (*Crimson Empire* #6 [Dark Horse]) (Internet exclusive)
- 02: Darth Vader & Rebel Officer (*Star Wars* #1* [Marvel])
- 03: Governor Tarkin & Stormtrooper (*Star Wars* #2* [Marvel])
- 04: Chewbacca & Han Solo (*Star Wars* #3* [Marvel])
- 05: Quinlan Vos & Vilmarh Grahrk (*Star Wars* #19 ["Twilight" 1 of 4]; [Dark Horse])
- 06: Luke Skywalker & R2-D2 (*Star Wars* #4 [Marvel])
- 07: Obi-Wan Kenobi & ARC Trooper Alpha (*Star Wars* #55 ["Republic"]; [Dark Horse])
- 08: A'sharad Hett & The Dark Woman (*Star Wars*

#31 ["The Hunt for Aurra Sing" 4 of 4]; [Dark Horse])
- 09: Leia Organa & Darth Vader (*The Empire Strikes Back: Infinities* #4 [Dark Horse])
- 10: Mara Jade & Luke Skywalker (*Heir to the Empire* #1 [Dark Horse]))
- 11: Anakin Skywalker & Assassin Droid (*Star Wars* #52 ["Republic"]; [Dark Horse])
- 12: Baron Fel & Derek "Hobbie" Klivian (*X-Wing: Rogue Squadron* #21 [Dark Horse]))
- 13: Koffi Arana & Bultar Swan (*Purge* #1 [w/ trade paperback cover] [Dark Horse])
- 14: Lt. Jundland & Deena Shan (*Empire* #39 [Dark Horse])
- 15: Mouse & Basso in Disguise (*Empire* #37 [Dark Horse])
- 16: Clone Commando & Super Battle Droid (*Star Wars Tales* #23 [Dark Horse])

NOTE: In the reprinted Marvel Comic included within these comic packs, Hasbro decided to replace the artwork of few select comic frames with scans of the action figures included with the comic pack: they swapped out the illustration with a scan of the toy (!).

2007

» **(WALMART EXCLUSIVES)**
- Boba Fett & RA-7 Droid (*Star Wars* #81 [Marvel])
- Commander Keller & Galactic Marine (*Star Wars* #79 ["Republic"]; [Dark Horse])
- Obi-Wan Kenobi & Bail Organa (*Revenge of the Sith* #4 [Dark Horse])

» **2008 (WALMART EXCLUSIVES)**
- Count Dooku & Anakin Skywalker (*Revenge of the Sith* #1 [Dark Horse])
- Kashyyyk Trooper & Wookiee Warrior (*Revenge of the Sith* #3 [Dark Horse])
- Lando Calrissian & Stormtrooper (*Star Wars* #44 [revised cover] [Marvel])

Evolutions

- Anakin Skywalker to Darth Vader [repack of 2005's *ROTS* set of the same name]
  - *Anakin Skywalker—Jedi Hero* (Attack of the Clones)
  - *Anakin Skywalker—Clone Wars Commander* (Revenge of the Sith)
  - *Darth Vader—Evil Sith Lord* (A New Hope)
- Clone Trooper to Stormtrooper [repack of 2005's *ROTS* set #2 of the same name (with gray-toned paint applications)]
  - *Clone Trooper—The Clone Wars* (Attack of the Clones)
  - *Clone Trooper—The Fall of the Republic* (Revenge of the Sith)
  - *Stormtrooper [Sandtooper]—The Rebellion* (A New Hope)
- The Sith [repack of 2005's *ROTS* set of the same name]
  - *Darth Maul—The Sith Return* (The Phantom Menace)
  - *Count Dooku—The Clone Wars* (Attack of the Clones)
  - *Emperor Palpatine—The Republic Falls* (Revenge of the Sith)
- The Fett Legacy
  - *Mandalore—Knights of the Old Republic*
  - *Jango Fett—Attack of the Clones*
  - *Boba Fett—The Empire Strikes Back*
- The Jedi Legacy
  - *Qui-Gon Jinn—The Phantom Menace*
  - *Bultar Swan—Attack of the Clones*
  - *Luke Skywalker—New Jedi Order*
- The Sith Legacy
  - *Darth Nihilus—Knights of the Old Republic*
  - *Darth Bane—The Old Republic*
  - *Darth Maul—The Phantom Menace*
- Vader's Secret Apprentice

- » *Secret Apprentice [Starkiller]* (Star Wars: The Force Unleashed)
- » *Sith Lord* (Star Wars: The Force Unleashed)
- » *Jedi Knight* (Star Wars: The Force Unleashed)

Exclusives

- » (CELEBRATION IV / CELEBRATION EUROPE)
  - McQuarrie Signature Series: Concept Luke Skywalker (with exclusive Collector Coin)
  - McQuarrie Signature Series: Concept R2-D2 & C-3PO (with exclusive Collector Coin)
- » (STAR WARS WEEKENDS 2007 [WALT DISNEY WORLD])
  - Cantina Band Member (with Lights and Music) [repack of *Episode IV*: The Modal Nodes Cantina Band* (Walmart exclusive) from the TAC 2007's Commemorative Tin Collection]—five figures are available, each with a unique accessory, none of the characters' names are on the package: Diokk Na'ts [with Dorenian Beshniquel/Fizz], Figrin D'an (with Klo Horn), Ickabel G'ont [with Fanfar], Nalan Cheel [with Bandfill], with Tech Mo'r [with Omni Box].
- » (SAN DIEGO COMIC-CON INTERNATIONAL)
  - McQuarrie Signature Series: Concept Obi-Wan Kenobi & Yoda (with exclusive Collector Coin)
  - R2-KT (Shared Exclusive)—solicited for charity (the card front text reads: "In loving memory of Katie Johnson, Hasbro and Lucasfilm Ltd. Are proud to support the Make-A-Wish Foundation")
  - Shadow Scout (with Speeder Bike)
- » (STARWARSSHOP.COM)
  - Concept General Grievous (with exclusive Collector's Coin)
  - Shadow Troopers (Jedi-Con 2008 & StarWarsShop.com)
- » (THE FORCE UNLEASHED)
  - Stormtrooper Commander (GameStop [pre-order with game])

- Darth Vader & Incinerator Troopers (Walmart)
    » *Darth Vader*
    » *Incinerator Trooper (x2)*
- Star Wars: The Force Unleashed Commemorative Collection (Walmart)
    » *Emperor Palpatine*
    » *Shadow Stormtrooper (x2)*

Collector Coins

- 2007 Vintage Coin Set (mail-away). Includes the following items:
    » *Display Box*
    » *Bossk (Bounty Hunter) Collector Coin*
    » *Han Solo (Rebel Leader) Collector Coin*
    » *IG-88 (Bounty Hunter) Collector Coin*
    » *Luke Skywalker (Jedi Apprentice) Collector Coin*
    » *Princess Leia (Rebel General) Collector Coin*
    » *Snowtrooper (Galactic Empire) Collector Coin, and the (once) hard-to-find*
    » *Toy Fair 2007 Collector Coin*
- Toy Fair Exclusive Collector Coin (available at the 2007 International Toy Fair until the release of the 2007 "Vintage Coin Set" [above])

Multi-Packs

» [COMMEMORATIVE TIN COLLECTIONS]
EPISODE I: THE PHANTOM MENACE (1 OF 6)
- Collectible Tin
- Darth Maul
- Obi-Wan Kenobi
- Qui-Gon Jinn
- R2-R9

EPISODE II: ATTACK OF THE CLONES (2 OF 6)
- Anakin Skywalker
- Clone Trooper (Lieutenant)
- Collectible Tin
- Count Dooku
- Jango Fett

EPISODE III: REVENGE OF THE SITH (3 OF 6)
- Anakin Skywalker
- AT-RT Driver
- Collectible Tin
- Mace Windu
- Yoda
- Episode IV: A New Hope (4 of 6)
- C-3PO
- Collectible Tin
- Darth Vader
- Princess Leia
- Sandtrooper

EPISODE V: EMPIRE STRIKES BACK (5 OF 6)
- Collectible Tin
- Chewbacca (Hoth)
- Collectible Tin
- Han Solo (Hoth)
- Luke Skywalker (Hoth)
- Snowtrooper (Hoth)

EPISODE VI: RETURN OF THE JEDI (6 OF 6)
- Collectible Tin
- Darth Vader
- Princess Leia (Endor)
- Rebel Commando
- Scout Trooper

EPISODE IV: THE MODAL NODES CANTINA BAND*
(Walmart exclusive)
- Modal Node member (x5)

Although there are a total of <u>seven</u> members of The Modal Nodes (Doikk Na'ts, Figrin D'an, Ickabel G'ont, Lirin Car'n, Tech Mo'r, Tedn Dahai, and Nalan Cheel), only five of them are included in this multi-pack.

EPISODE II: ATTACK OF THE CLONES (Kmart exclusive)
- » *Collectible Tin*
- » *Mace Windu*
- » *Oppo Rancisis*
- » *Sora Bulq*
- » *Zam Wesell*

EPISODE III: REVENGE OF THE SITH (Kmart exclusive)
- » *Anakin Skywalker*
- » *Clone Commander Cody*
- » *Clone Pilot*
- » *Collectible Tin*
- » *General Grievous*

EPISODE VI: A NEW HOPE (Kmart exclusive)
- » *Biker Scout*
- » *Collectible Tin*
- » *Darth Vader*
- » *Death Star Gunner*
- » *R5-J2*

» (EXCLUSIVES)
- "I Am Your Father's Day" [Sunday, June 17, 2007] gift pack (Walmart)
  - » *Darth Vader*
  - » *Father's Day Card*
  - » *Gift Box*
  - » *Luke Skywalker*
- Republic Elite Forces: Mandalorians & Clone Troopers (Entertainment Earth)
  - » *ARC Trooper (x2)*
  - » *Clone Trooper (x2)*
  - » *Dred Priest*

- » *Isabet Reau*
- » *Mij Gilamar*
- Republic Elite Forces: Mandalorians & Omega Squad (Entertainment Earth)
  - » *B'Arin Apma*
  - » *Llats Ward*
  - » *Omega Squad (x4)*
  - » *Rav Bralor*
- *Star Wars: Battlefront II*—Clone Pack (Previews Exclusive)—sold in conjunction with the Droid Pack
  - » *Clone Engineer*
  - » *Clone Sharpshooter*
  - » *Clone Trooper*
  - » *Heavy Trooper*
  - » *Galactic Marine*
  - » *Jet Trooper*
- *Star Wars: Battlefront II*—Droid Pack (Previews Exclusive) —sold in conjunction with the Clone Pack
  - » *Ammunition Droid*
  - » *Assassin Battle Droid*
  - » *Assault Battle Droid*
  - » *Destroyer Droid*
  - » *Engineer Battle Droid*
  - » *Magnaguard Droid*
  - » *Super Battle Droid*
- The Max Rebo Band: Jabba's Palace Entertainers (Walmart)
  - » *Greeata*
  - » *Joh Yowza*
  - » *Lyn Me*
  - » *Rappertunie*
  - » *Rystáll*

- The Max Rebo Band: Jabba's Palace Musicians (Walmart)
  - » *Barquin D'an*
  - » *Doda Bodonawieedo*
  - » *Droopy McCool*
  - » *Max Rebo*
  - » *Sy Snootles*

TAC, "Order 66" packaging (2007-2008)

When Emperor Palpatine sent a holographic transmission to his loyal troops, as leader of the Grand Army of the Republic, he triggered a command — Order 66 — programmed into a biochip implanted into the soldiers' brains during their development as members of the GAR's clone army. According to the 3rd novel of the *Republic Commando* series written by Karen Traviss (titled *Republic Commando: True Colors*), the insidious Order 66 states: "In the event of Jedi officers acting against the interests of the Republic, and after receiving specific orders verified as coming directly from the Supreme Commander (Chancellor), GAR commanders will remove those officers by lethal force, and command of the GAR will revert to the Supreme Commander (Chancellor) until a new command structure is established." The action figures released in this assortment were based on the characters involved in this implementation of this order.

» ORDER 66

(SERIES 1—2007)
- 1 of 6: Emperor and Shock Trooper Commander
- 2 of 6: Mace Windu and Galactic Marine
- 3 of 6: Darth Vader and Commander Bow
- 4 of 6: Anakin Skywalker and Airborne Trooper
- 5 of 6: Obi-Wan Kenobi and Utapau AT-RT Driver
- 6 of 6: Yoda and Kashyyyk Trooper

(SERIES 2—2008)
- 1 of 6: Obi-Wan Kenobi and ARC Trooper Commander
- 2 of 6: Anakin Skywalker and ARC Trooper
- 3 of 6: Tsui Choi and BARC Trooper
- 4 of 6: Emperor Palpatine and Commander Vill
- 5 of 6: Luminara Unduli and AT-RT Driver
- 6 of 6: Master Sev and ARC Trooper

» VEHICLES
- AT-TP Walker
- Anakin's Jedi Starfighter (Coruscant) [yellow-colored]
- Anakin's Jedi Starfighter (Mustafar) [green-colored]
- Darth Vader's Sith Starfighter
- Darth Vader's TIE Advanced Starfighter x1
- General Grievous' Starfighter
- Hailfire Droid
- Mace Windu's Jedi Starfighter
- Obi-Wan's Jedi Starfighter (Coruscant) [maroon-colored]
- Obi-Wan's Jedi Starfighter (Utapau) [blue-colored]
- Saesee Tiin's Jedi Starfighter (Clone Wars)
- Sith Infiltrator
- TIE Fighter
- Trade Federation Armored Assault Tank (AAT)
- V-wing Starfighter

» (TOYS"R"US EXCLUSIVES)
- Elite TIE Interceptor (with 181st Squadron TIE Pilot)
- Obi-Wan Kenobi's Jedi Starfighter with Hyperspace Ring
- Y-wing Fighter (with Y-wing Pilot [Lt. Lepira], and R5-F7)

» (TARGET EXCLUSIVES)
- Aayla Secura's Jedi Starfighter

- ARC-170 Fighter (Clone Wars deco)
- TIE Bomber

» VINTAGE FIGURES
- Bossk (Bounty Hunter)
- Han Solo (Hoth Outfit)

- IG-88 (Bounty Hunter)
- Luke Skywalker (Bespin Fatigues)
- Princess Leia Organa (in Combat Poncho)
- Imperial Stormtrooper (Hoth Battle Gear)

Obi-Wan Kenobi's Jedi Starfighter with Hyperspace Ring, 2007, 30th Anniversary Collection, *[Attack of the Clones]* (Toys"R"Us exclusive), **$40-$52 MIB**. One of the more interesting exclusives offered during the past thirty+ years, Obi-Wan Kenobi's Jedi Starfighter with Hyperspace Ring includes an essential vehicle-based accessory that collectors should recognize as an exceedingly valuable commodity. Purchasing this Toys"R"Us exclusive guarantees that you'll obtain a Hyperspace Ring which will attach to the nose of any Delta Starfighter of your choice—not just the one included in this box. Prominently featured in *Attack of the Clones*, this accoutrement allows Jedi Starfighters the ability to travel vast distances since the vehicle did not come equipped with a hyperdrive. The ring will fit on any model of Delta-7 Aethersprite-class light interceptor or Delta-7B Aethersprite-class light interceptor.

CHAPTER 14

Saga Legends

Due to the overwhelming success of Hasbro's 30th Anniversary Collection, the company decided to take advantage of the sub-line's triumph. Debuting in April of 2007 and running until 2008, the line ran concurrent to the 30th Anniversary Collection — with some packaging samples and action figures appearing almost interchangeably due to similarities in design and manufacture. Regardless, every single action figure released in Saga Legends was a straight re-pack of a previously solicited character from many of the previous Hasbro *Star Wars* assortments. Like their sister line, each figure came with a chromed Collector Coin*, while the Saga Legends' final three series of releases (16 total figures) sported a "Fan's Choice" label on the toy packaging—all of the characters were selected via an online voting ballot maintained by the revered *Star Wars* website Rebelscum.com. The last two noteworthy elements of this sub-line: 1) none of the figures sported a number, and 2) there was a wealth of running changes made to the many "troop builders" released under the Saga Legends banner: from re-colored paint applications signifying different Imperial ranks to revised and replaced accessories to even a newly-minted head sculpt, this line still remains quite popular on the secondary market.

Although the 2007 and early 2008 packaging for Saga Legends imitated 30th Anniversary packaging, the packaging changed in July 2008, when the action figure card backs were produced to imitate the look and feel of a Stormtrooper helmet (albeit rendered in black, blue,

Imperial Officer (variant head sculpt #3), 2007, Saga Legends [*Empire Strikes Back*], **$10-$14 MOC, $6-$9 MLC** (left); Imperial Officer (variant head sculpt #2—blond hair), 2007, Saga Legends [*Empire Strikes Back*], **$10-$14 MOC, $6-$9 MLC** (right).

and white). The line would endure until 2011, and would return to retail pegs in 2013.

*Note #1: The Collector Coins included within Saga Legends packages were rarely character-specific: nearly every action figure included a coin that indicated the film in which the character-in-question appeared. So then, there were six main silver-plated coins indicating *Episodes I-VI*. Also, a gold-plated coin was packed with Expanded Universe-based characters.

Note #2: The designs of the "bonus Pit Droids" released in this sub-line were based upon the droids solicited in countries (other than the U.S.) who refused to participate in the Episode I "CommTech Chip" promotion. Instead of packing a CommTech Chip inside the packages of Episode I characters, a Pit Droid figure was included as a bonus.

2007

- 501st Clone Trooper [#1] [repaint of *ROTS* 2005's #65 Tactical Ops Trooper (Vader's Legion)]
- 501st Clone Trooper [#2] [repaint of *ROTS* 2005's #41 Clone Trooper (Super Articulated!)—with clean armor]
- Battle Droids (2-pack #1; tan infantry & commander) [repaints of the Battle Droid included in Saga 2002's Deluxe C-3PO's (Droid Factory Assembly Line)]
- Battle Droid (2-pack #2; maroon blaster damage & lightsaber damage) [repaints of the Battle Droid included in Saga 2002's Deluxe C-3PO's (Droid Factory Assembly Line)]
- Battle Droid (2-pack #3; tan blaster damage & lightsaber damage) [repaints of the Battle Droid included in Saga 2002's Deluxe C-3PO's (Droid Factory Assembly Line)]
- Battle Droid (2-pack #4; tan dirty & clean) [repaints of the Battle Droid included in Saga 2002's Deluxe C-3PO's (Droid Factory Assembly Line)]

C-3PO (with Battle Droid head), 2007, Saga Legends [*Episode II: Attack of the Clones*], **$6-$8 MOC, $4-$6 MLC**. A repack of The Saga Collection's C-3PO (Droid Factory Assembly Line) from 2006, this popular character was reissued in Saga Legends, allowing kids and fans alike to reenact the moment when the loquacious droid's head is replaced with that of a Battle Droid in *Episode II: Attack of the Clones*.

- Biker Scout [repack of VTSC 2006's Biker Scout]
- Boba Fett [repack of VOTC 2004's Boba Fett]
- C-3PO (with Battle Droid head) [repack of TSC 2006's C-3PO (Droid Factory Assembly Line)]
- Chewbacca [repack of *ROTS* 2005's #05 Chewbacca (Wookie Rage!)]
- Clone Commander (Coruscant) [repack of *ROTS* 2005's Clone Trooper to Stormtrooper *Evolutions* set)]
- Clone Trooper (*Attack of the Clones*) [repack of OTC 2005's Clone Trooper Troop Builder 4-pack]

- Clone Trooper (*Revenge of the Sith*) [repaint of *ROTS* 2005's #41 Clone Trooper (Super Articulated!)]
- Clone Trooper Officer (Captain) [repack of OTC 2005's Clone Trooper Troop Builder 4-pack]
- Clone Trooper Officer (Commander) [repack of OTC 2005's Clone Trooper Troop Builder 4-pack]
- Clone Trooper Officer (Lieutenant) [repack of OTC 2005's Clone Trooper Troop Builder 4-pack]
- Clone Trooper Officer (Sergeant) [repack of OTC 2005's Clone Trooper Troop Builder 4-Pack (green paint applications) Entertainment Earth exclusive]
- Darth Maul [repack of *Episode I* 1999's Sith Speeder and Darth Maul]
- Darktrooper (Fan's Choice #1) [repack of POTF II 1998's Dark Trooper]
- Darth Vader [repack of TSC 2006's #038 Darth Vader]
- Darth Vader (Anakin Skywalker) [repack of TSC 2006's #025 Anakin Skywalker]
- Destroyer Droid [repack of *ROTS* 2005's #44 Destroyer Droid (Firing Arm-Blaster!)]
- General Grievous [repack of *ROTS* 2005's #09 General Grievous (Four Lightsaber Attack!)]
- Imperial Officer (variant head sculpt #1) [repack of POTJ 2001's Imperial Officer with new head sculpt]
- Imperial Officer (variant head sculpt #2—blond hair) [repack of Saga 2002's Imperial Officer]
- Imperial Officer (variant head sculpt #3) [repack of the 2nd version of Saga 2002's Imperial Officer]
- Obi-Wan Kenobi [repack of the body of *ROTS* 2005's #55 Obi-Wan Kenobi (With Pilot Gear!) & the repainted head of TSC 2006's #028 Obi-Wan Kenobi]
- Pit Droids (2-pack #1; white—with Power Convertor) [repaints of 1999, Euro-exclusive "bonus Pit Droid" figures]

RA-7, 2007, Saga Legends [*Episode IV: A New Hope*], **$8-$12 MOC**, **$6-$8 MLC**. Taken right out of the Original Trilogy Collection's deluxe Jawa Sandcrawler vehicle and figure set (a Diamond Comic Previews exclusive), this version of RA-7 could be found individually carded in the Saga Legends sub-line for the first time ever. However, although this protocol droid lacks poseability, its toy more than makes up for this with authenticity of design: RA-7 is Arakyd Industries' iconic "Death Star Droid." This spectacularly-rendered action figure was based upon the character that a disabled R2-D2 encountered within the bowels of a massive Sandcrawler in *Episode IV*.

- Pit Droids (2-pack #2; brown—with Power Convertor) [repaints of 1999, Euro-exclusive "bonus Pit Droid" figures]
- Pit Droids (2-pack #3; orange—with Power Convertor) [repaints of 1999, Euro-exclusive "bonus Pit Droid" figures]
- Pit Droids (2-pack #4; white—with Storage Locker) [repaints of 1999, Euro-exclusive "bonus Pit Droid" figures]

- Pit Droids (2-pack #5; brown—with Storage Locker) [repaints of 1999, Euro-exclusive "bonus Pit Droid" figures]
- Pit Droids (2-pack #6; orange—with Storage Locker) [repaints of 1999, Euro-exclusive "bonus Pit Droid" figures]
- Princess Leia (Boushh disguise) [repack of TSC 2006's #001 Princess Leia (Boushh Disguise)]
- R2-D2 [repack of *ROTS* 2005's #48 R2-D2 (Electronic Lights and Sounds!)]
- R4-I9 [repack of Saga 2003's R4-19 from Imperial Forces (Toys"R"Us exclusive) multi-pack]
- RA-7 [repack of OTC 2004's RA-7 from the Jawa Sandcrawler (Diamond Comic Previews exclusive)]
- Saesee Tiin [repack of TSC 2006's Jedi vs. Sidious Battle Pack]
- Sandtrooper (#1; "Super Dirty" Sergeant—body #1) [repaint of TSC 2006's #037 Sandtrooper]
- Sandtrooper (#2; "Dirty" Squad Leader—body #1) [repaint of TSC 2006's #037 Sandtrooper]
- Sandtrooper (#3; "Clean" Corporal—body #1) [repaint of TSC 2006's #037 Sandtrooper]
- Sandtrooper (#4; "Clean" Sergeant—body #1) [repaint of TSC 2006's #037 Sandtrooper]
- Sandtrooper (#5; "Dirty" Sergeant—body #2) [repack of figure #2 from *ROTS* 2005's Clone Trooper to Stormtrooper *Evolutions* set)]
- Sandtrooper (#6; "Less Dirty" Squad Leader—body #2) [repack of figure #2 from *ROTS* 2005's Clone Trooper to Stormtrooper *Evolutions* set)]
- Shock Trooper [repack of TSC 2006's Skirmish at the Senate Battle Pack]
- TC-14 (repack of *Episode I* 1999's TC-14)
- Yoda [repack of *ROTS* 2005's #03 Yoda (Firing Cannon!)]